Who's Buying You?

Mack Story

DEDICATION

To all of those who choose to sell with integrity.
In memory of a true sales professional, Matt Lynott.

CONTENTS

ACKNOWLEDGMENTS

I would like to thank the salespeople I've encountered throughout my life who simply tried to help me get what I wanted...whether they had it or not. It was a pleasure doing business with you all. I've referred you and mentioned you to others many times.

1

THE FOUNDATION OF SELLING

WHEN YOU INCREASE YOUR INFLUENCE, YOU WILL INCREASE YOUR SALES

"If you work hard on your job you can make a living. But, if you work hard on yourself, you can make a fortune." ~ Jim Rohn

Influence is the foundation of selling. If you have enough influence, you will get the sale. If you don't, you won't. If you have enough influence, you will get referrals. If you don't, you won't. If you have enough influence, you will get repeat customers. If you don't, you won't. As Bob Burg said, *"All things being equal, people will do business with and refer business to those people they know, like, and trust."*

Everything in sales rises and falls on influence. With influence, you will thrive. Without it, you will take a dive.

When someone buys from you, you have successfully influenced them to make two purchases. They first buy YOU. Then, they buy the product or service from you.

The lessons and principles found on the pages of this book are meant to motivate and inspire you to work hard on yourself. As a result, you will increase your positive influence in all situations and with everyone. If you do, your *"fortune"* will follow. If you don't, someone else will enjoy your piece of the sales pie. The old saying *"If you snooze, you lose."* comes to mind.

Influence is what I'm passionate about. I'll begin by

sharing with you what truly qualifies me to write this little book on sales. Everything I read about, write about, think about, and speak about relates to principles of character-based, positive influence. Or as it applies to sales, it's all about integrity and character-based selling. I define leadership as one of my mentors, John C. Maxwell, defines leadership, *"Leadership is influence."*

In 2008, I committed to becoming a lifetime student of character-based, positive influence. As a result, I have multiplied my hourly rate since then by a factor of 228. That's based on what I was earning per hour in 2008 compared to what I have earned for my best hour since then. And, my rates continue to climb.

Let me simplify this a bit more to reveal how my character multiplied my competency. From 1988 to 2008, 20 years of working hard on my job, my hourly rate increased five times while gaining experience in my field (competency) and earning a college degree (more competency) which was required for better jobs. From 2008 to 2017, less than 10 years of working hard on myself, my hourly rate has increased 228 times while focusing only on learning and applying character-based principles of influence. I learned how to sell MYSELF.

Don't miss it. My result to date is: 5 X 228 = 1,140.

I want to help you achieve amazing results too, but you've got to do the hard work on yourself as Jim Rohn stated so well. My intent is to help you learn to use *who you are* to leverage *what you know*.

In the context of sales, I have received strong five figure speaking fees to speak on the subject of influence. I don't consider myself a sales professional. However, I am an influence professional. Or in my terms, I'm a leadership professional. By influencing others to pay many thousands of dollars to hear me speak, I have become an expert in selling my most important product: ME. We are all selling something. The first and most important thing we *must* all sell is ourselves.

You must develop your competency. But, that is only a small part of the equation as Napoleon Hill explains here, *"The average person who wanted to get an education would probably think first of some college or university, with the false belief that these institutions could 'educate' their students...Don't believe for a moment that you can buy an education for money. You can't do it. An education is something you have to work for. Furthermore, it cannot be acquired in the usual four years given over to college training. If we are good students, we are going to school always. We never get through. Life is one continuous school, and the kind of students we are depends upon the kind of work we do as we go through this great university."*

A four year degree may take you to the base of the mountain of success, but it will take a lifetime of growth and development to get you to the top. If you're not yet a student of leadership (influence), I hope after reading this book you will become one.

Leadership is influence, and influence sells.

SELLER BEWARE

1. You must increase your influence in order to increase your sales. More influence leads to more options!
2. You must intentionally work hard on yourself, not your job, to reach your full potential. Be more!
3. Your competency will take you part of the way, but it is your character that will take you all of the way.

2

SELLER BEWARE

TODAY, BUYERS ARE OFTEN MORE INFORMED THAN SELLERS

"Sales persuasion and influence, moving others, has changed more in the last 10 years than it has in the last 100 years. It has transitioned from buyer beware to seller beware." ~ Daniel Pink

"It's no longer buyer beware. Today, it's seller beware." I remember when I first heard Daniel Pink speak these words several years ago. They stuck with me.

At the time, I had never considered writing a book for sales professionals. After all, I don't consider myself a fan of, or knowledgeable about, popular selling or marketing techniques and practices. However, I am highly effective when it comes to influencing people based on my character, my ability to quickly connect with them, my ability to build trust, and my ability to make them feel valued. In other words, *I can sell myself.*

To be completely transparent, I don't look forward to meeting, interacting, or dealing with salespeople who have been trained on and have bought into the personality-based techniques and practices of *how to appear to be* instead of focusing on character-based principles related to *how to actually be.*

Everything I read about, learn about, teach about, and speak about is related to character-based development. Daniel's words resonated with me. They have been on my mind since that very day, *"It's no longer buyer beware. Today, it's seller beware."*

Since hearing those words, I have shared them many times with sales professionals. Why? Because I like to help people excel, reach their goals, unleash their potential, and make things happen for themselves and for their families.

There's no denying it. Today, the buyer does have the advantage over the seller. Not sometime, every time. Most often, the buyer is holding their advantage in their hand. It's called a smart phone.

Today, the buyer can connect to the internet and learn everything about your product and your competition before they ever meet you and hear your well-rehearsed sales pitch. Actually, depending on your product and your marketing methods, they may be able to experience your sales pitch and your style on video before they ever meet you. The quality, and *what they feel about you* while watching the video, will determine if you actually get to meet them or if you never get to meet them.

Today, the buyer's first impression of you may very well be your online presence or your lack of an online presence. They can often read reviews by other buyers who have experience with your company, your product, and yes, sometimes even with you. They can also stalk you on various social media platforms to see who you *really* are when you're not trying to sell something.

Today, the buyer can compare features and prices instantly. Maybe while they are standing in front of you. In many cases, they will let you invest your time showing and demonstrating the product. Then, they will choose to bypass you altogether by purchasing from someone else or by purchasing online.

I'm sure you get the point by now and can reflect on

your own experiences and quickly agree. Today, the buyer absolutely has the advantage on all fronts.

The one major advantage you still have is YOU!

IF they like you. *IF* they trust you. *IF* they feel you want to help them. *IF* they want to buy from you. *IF* they want to speak positively about you to others. And *IF* they do, it's all because of YOU. You are the key to your success.

This book will provide unique insights in bite-size pieces to help you leverage your advantage, not over the buyer, but over your competition: those who are selling what you're selling and trying to steal your buyers.

My purpose on these pages is to help you sell yourself, not your products. Until you're able to sell yourself effectively, you won't have to worry too much about selling your products. As Ralph Marston said, *"Truly appreciate those around you, and you'll soon find many others around you."* The more people you attract, the more product you will sell. *Word of mouth* sells.

SELLER BEWARE

1. *Your customers are better informed today than they have ever been. Your character is your advantage!*

2. *You can't compete with those who are online if you're not online. Think about your marketing methods!*

3. *Your real competition is the character of those who are selling what you're selling. YOU are the advantage!*

3

WORD OF MOUTH

WHAT ARE THE PEOPLE YOU MEET SAYING ABOUT YOU?

"The more valuable you become, the more the marketplace will reward you. Give first. Become known as a resource, not a salesperson. Your value is linked to your knowledge and your willingness to help others." ~ Jeffrey Gitomer

When it comes to spreading the word about a product or service, everyone knows there is nothing more effective than *word of mouth advertising*. When others endorse a product with enthusiasm and passion, tell us what they love about it, and tell us why we've just got to have it, we are far more likely to consider making a purchase than if we're exposed to traditional advertising about a product or service.

Word of mouth is even more effective when people are not satisfied. Most often, if we hear just one bad review, we immediately start looking at alternative products or providers. We truly pay attention when someone shares about a bad experience with a product, service, or a salesperson.

Word of mouth advertising will always trump other forms of advertising. Why? Because we trust those we know much more than we trust those we don't know.

You don't have any control over the *word of mouth* advertising about the product you're selling. The perceived value, quality, and performance of the product will determine what people are saying about it. The design, engineering, and manufacturing teams are responsible for that.

This book isn't about products. It's about people because everyone makes their money selling a product, a service, or themselves. Everyone is selling something.

As you read the rest of this book, forget about products and services. What you need to consider and think about is simply this: *word of mouth* advertising applies to YOU too. ALL the people who interact with you, personally and professionally, will have an opinion of you. That opinion matters. And, if you're a salesperson, it matters a lot!

Here's why. As John C. Maxwell stated so well, *"One of the worst mistakes a person can make is to think they are working for someone else. They may be getting paid by someone else. But, they are working for themselves."* I totally agree and dedicated an entire chapter to helping others understand this key principle of success in my book, *MAXIMIZE Your Potential: Unleashing the LEADER Within.*

If you're selling for free, then you *are* working for someone else because they are benefiting financially, and you're not. But, if you're selling with the expectation of being paid to sell, then you are absolutely working for yourself. YOU *are* in business for yourself. When you understand this principle, *word of mouth* becomes even more important. It's impacting your business: YOU.

YOU are now the primary product that must be sold. YOU are the sole salesperson. YOU can be referred by many, but YOU can only be sold by one. You are 100% responsible for the perceived value, quality, and performance of the most important product you'll ever sell: YOURSELF.

This entire book is based on this one simple principle: YOU *are* working for yourself. Your sales will rise or fall based on your ability to influence other people.

People who never plan to buy from you will have an opinion of YOU. People who don't have a need for your product can and will provide good or bad *word of mouth* for you. People who you meet only once may advertise for you. People you socialize with but don't sell to will have an opinion of YOU. Those who consider buying from you will have an opinion of you. Those who do buy your products or services will have an opinion of YOU.

What will all of these people say about YOU?

I have no idea, but what I do know is this. Who YOU *are* will determine most, if not all, of what they say. They may not always remember what you said or what you did. But, they won't forget how you made them feel. That feeling will influence the *word of mouth* feedback you receive from them.

People are sensitive creatures. I know, you're probably tough, but you can easily validate this principle. How did the last person you were with make you feel? How did your boss make you feel? How did the last salesperson make you feel? Now, the two most important questions. How did you make them feel? Do you care? I hope so because they will all be providing you with *word of mouth*. I hope it's all good, but it's not up to me. It's up to YOU!

SELLER BEWARE

1. You determine your own word of mouth advertising. It will either make you or break you. Think about it!

2. You are selling yourself 24 hours a day, 7 days a week, 365 days a year. You're never closed!

3. Every person you ever meet will form an opinion about your business: YOU! Will they refer you or reject you?

4

WHO'S BUYING YOU?

UNTIL YOU SELL YOURSELF, YOU WON'T SELL MUCH

"When you decide to pursue greatness, you are taking responsibility for your life. This means you are choosing to accept the consequences of your actions, and to become the agent of your mental, physical, spiritual, and material success. You may not always be able to control what life puts in your path, but I believe you can always control who you are."
~ Les Brown

I want to help you win by helping you sell yourself. Everything you will learn throughout this book is intended to help you intentionally create more positive *word of mouth*. When you do this, you will win at a much higher level and for a much longer time.

However, there's one thing I can't help you with. It's critical to effectively making the sale. I'm referring to passion. If you're going to earn your money selling, you need to stack the odds in your favor. Passion is a must.

Passion sells. Are you passionate? Are you passionate about the product or service you're selling and the company you're selling it for? If not, you have a significant disadvantage when compared to someone who can answer with an authentic *"Yes!"* If you're not passionate about what you're selling, you're either selling the wrong product or working at the wrong company.

Why would you create such a disadvantage for yourself? You're losing sales and dollars whether you know it or not. Make a course correction as soon as possible. Having a passion for the product and the company will give you an edge over those who don't. As Dan Burns said so well, *"Find your passion and wrap your career around it."* If you do, everything else will take care of itself.

Imagine you're considering buying from two salespeople at two different companies selling a similar product. You're happy with either product and either brand. It's no longer about the product. It's now about the salesperson. You're actually happy with both of them too. As far as you're concerned, they are both exceptional in all areas except in the area of passion. One is neutral and seems to care less if you actually buy the product. The other has you so fired up you're thinking about buying two, and you now believe everyone else needs one also.

Everything is the same, except the salesperson's passion for the product and the company. Who do you buy from? Who do you give positive *word of mouth*? Who gets no *word of mouth*? Or worse, who gets negative *word of mouth*?

The one who lost the sale may never know why. They won't get referrals in the future and won't hear the bad *word of mouth* after the sale was lost. Missed sales due to lack of passion simply may never be known. For the loser, the thought may be that business is just slow.

Lack of passion can cost you short term and long term. I'm sure Reggie Leach had passion in mind when he said, *"Success is not the result of spontaneous combustion. You must first set yourself on fire."* Passion fuels the fire.

Success doesn't begin with making the sale. Success

begins before the sale. Success begins with who you are and why you do what you do. I believe sales guru Jeffrey Gitomer nailed it when he said, *"Many salespeople believe that customers buy their products and services first. Incorrect. The first thing prospects buy is the salesperson. The first sale made is you."*

Most often, in order to sell yourself, you must get everything right. When it comes to selling yourself, one area of weakness can, and often will, cost you the sale.

My intent on the following pages is to help you think deeply about what it will take to truly get to the next level and beyond. For most people, it's not a lack of knowledge. It's a lack of awareness. As we begin to dig deeper together, I'm reminded of the great little poem titled *"Thinking"* by Walter D. Wintle:

"If you think you are beaten, you are; If you think you dare not, you don't; If you like to win, but think you can't, it is almost certain you won't. If you think you'll lose, you've lost. For out of the world, we find success begins with a fellow's will. It's all in the state of mind. If you think you're outclassed, you are. You've got to think high to rise. You've got to be sure of yourself before you can ever win a prize. Life's battles don't always go to the stronger or faster man; But sooner or later the man who wins is the man who thinks he can."

SELLER BEWARE

1. The first and most important thing you will sell is yourself. The sell starts long before the sale starts.
2. If you aren't passionate about the product you're selling, you're likely to lose the sale to someone who is.
3. Knowledge is important, but it's awareness that causes you to seek the appropriate knowledge.

5

WHY SHOULD I BUY FROM YOU?

THE UNSPOKEN QUESTION EVERY CUSTOMER WANTS ANSWERED

"People buy personalities as much as merchandise, and it is a question if they are not influenced more by the personalities with which they come in contact than they are by the merchandise." ~ Napoleon Hill

Why should I buy from YOU? What is it about YOU? I know you're a rock star. I get it. All salespeople believe they are rock stars. So, let's move past that. Or at least, let's break it down a bit because in the sales world, every team has a rock star: the salesperson with the most sales.

Rock star is a relative term. There's a BIG difference between being the best on your team, in your company, and in your industry. You may be a rock star on your team, but an unknown backup singer in your industry.

Don't make the mistake of measuring yourself against your peers. What do they have to do with you anyway? If you want a real challenge, do what the true rock stars in your industry do. Measure yourself against your potential.

Your potential is what you are truly capable of. Are you training to reach your potential like an Olympic athlete trains to win a gold medal? You against you.

You must decide how far you want to go. Sacrifice will be required. Give up habits that aren't serving you. Turn off the TV, quit playing games on your phone, stop surfing social media, and quit goofing off all weekend with too many cold beverages.

Create habits that will help you reach your goals. Get up early, stay up late, network like that's all you have to do, implement a personal development and growth plan, and get serious about making things happen for yourself. That's what true rock stars do.

Most salespeople, or anyone else for that matter, won't make the choices that will allow them to reach their potential. When you measure yourself against your potential, your scores drop tremendously. That's the score that reflects the truth about how you're really doing.

This brings us back to the question: Why would someone choose YOU over your competition?

As you ponder this simple but thought-provoking question, don't make the mistake of looking at yourself through rose colored *"seller"* glasses. It's the buyers who decide if they will buy from you or someone else. You can only influence their decision. You can't determine their decision. Therefore, you may want to look at the question again through the eyes of the buyer.

There is often a blind spot between us and the mirror. Stop and think about things from a buyer's perspective. Sure, you are in sales, but you are also a buyer. You make purchases just like the rest of us.

Consider the words of Ayn Rand, *"There is the man who wishes to be rich, but never thinks of discovering what means, actions, and conditions are required to achieve wealth."* If you haven't already read that last quote five times, stop and do it now. Do it slowly with intentional thought.

I hope you thought deeply about the last half of that quote. That's where the money is. This book is one example of *means*. There are many different means. But knowing how isn't enough. The means must result in definite *actions*. If the definite actions are right, you *will* create the right *conditions* that will allow you to achieve wealth. *Means*, *actions*, and *conditions*. You're responsible for all three. I can't do it for you, but everything I share in this book will help you make it happen.

Look at the following questions with *"buyer's"* glasses:

- *What do YOU look for in a salesperson?*
- *What makes a sales experience positive and memorable?*
- *What determines if you will refer a salesperson to family?*
- *What do you like about your favorite salesperson?*
- *What would you change about most salespeople?*

If you truly answered these questions using your *"buyer"* glasses, put your *"seller"* glasses back on and consider your answers. Can you honestly say you are the salesperson you just described? Whose interest do you primarily have in mind when selling? Yours or the buyer's? You will know it, but they will feel it.

If the customer is talking to you, they are interested in your product or service. But, that doesn't mean they were initially interested in buying from you. That's two completely different interests.

The mission is not to try and sell them something. The mission is to get them to want to buy something from YOU. Trust is the foundation of influence. Trust sells.

SELLER BEWARE

1. *You should measure yourself based on your potential, what you could and should be doing with your ability.*
2. *You are responsible for finding the means, taking the right actions, and creating the conditions for success.*
3. *You must become the salesperson everyone wants to buy from because of who you are, not how you are.*

6

ARE YOU TRUSTWORTHY?

IT'S ALL ABOUT WHO YOU ARE
AND WHAT YOU KNOW

"There is only one boss – the customer. He can fire everybody in the company from the chairman on down, simply by spending his money somewhere else."
~ Sam Walton

Strong words of truth from Sam Walton who became a mega-billionaire while helping many others become wealthy selling goods and services at Wal-Mart. Sam first sold himself. Then, he sold everything else and lots of it!

For salespeople, the boss is the last person they should ever worry about firing them. The boss will typically fire a salesperson only after many buyers have already fired them through their decisions not to buy from them. Many salespeople are fired every day by potential buyers, prospects as they call them.

Potential buyers literally fire you when they don't choose to buy from you. Some fire you after they meet you but before they buy from you. Some hire you (buy from you), and then fire you (never buy from you again). Worst of all, those who provide you with bad *word of mouth*, convince others to fire you before they ever even meet you.

When they're fired, far too many salespeople move on like it never even happened. *"You win some, you lose some."* they often say as if they had no responsibility at all in the buyer's decision to fire them. *"That's just the way it goes…"*

No reflection. No adjustment. No plan to change their results or to change their minds. By the way, your mind creates your results. If you want to change your results, you first must change your mind. Average salespeople tend not to *change their mind.* They do tend to continue to do a whole lot more of the same…day after day.

But, that's not you. How do I know? You're reading this little book to *change your mind.* You have already separated yourself from the masses of average salespeople. You're already exceptional because average people don't study *mind changing* books.

Now, let's consider the best buyers. They become your best customers. They don't just repeatedly buy from you. They also provide you with good *word of mouth* and convince others to hire you before they ever even meet you.

These referred buyers will hunt you down to buy from you. They're already sold on you. Don't you just love these types of buyers? This book is filled with information that will help you create more of these highly valuable buyers if you choose to apply what you're learning.

There's obviously a gap between being *"hired"* by a customer and being *"fired"* by a customer. At the most basic level, what creates the gap? It's pretty simple. Distrust. Trust closes what I call the *"Trust Gap."*

Trust is the foundation of influence. The more someone trusts you, the more influence you will have with them. The less someone trusts you, the less influence you will have with them. When it comes to buyers, high trust leads to *"hiring"* while low trust leads to *"firing."*

The question buyers ask and then answer for themselves about salespeople is this, *"Are you trustworthy?"*

They base their answer on who they *believe* you are and who they *perceive* you to be.

You can't make anyone trust you. If you could, no one would *"fire"* you. Everyone would trust you, and everyone would *"hire"* you. You would get every sale. As you already know, that's not how things work.

However, there is something you can intentionally do to close the Trust Gap. You can choose to become more and more trustworthy. Then, buyers will choose to trust or distrust you. Ultimately, buyers will decide whether or not they will trust you based on *who they are* and *what they value*.

There are two major components of trust: character and competency. There is only one chapter, the next one, dedicated to competency. The other 29 are related to helping you grow and develop your character.

There's something you should know about the trust equation that will put the importance of this book into perspective. Numerous research studies have shown that 87-90% of our influence comes from our character and 10-13% comes from our competency. That means, if you know *what* you're doing, there's only one thing holding you back. *How* you're doing it. Let that sink in.

Elbert Hubbard had this to say, *"Some men succeed by what they know; some by what they do; and a few by what they are."* When it comes to influence, it's about *who you are*.

SELLER BEWARE

1. Every person you interact with has the ability to get you hired or fired through word of mouth. Be smart!

2. Competency is important. What you know matters. However, character, who you are, matters most.

3. You leverage competency with character. Your character will launch you or limit you. Character sells!

7

DO YOUR HOMEWORK

THE CUSTOMER EXPECTS YOU TO KNOW WHAT YOU'RE TALKING ABOUT

"Standards of excellence are not chiseled in stone. They are constantly being redefined. It's important to recognize that what was graded as excellent last year may not be so this year. That is why we must keep mastering new skills." ~ Bobb Beihl

When it comes to building trust, it helps to know that all of us have an emotional trust account set up for each person we interact with. I first learned of this concept from Stephen R. Covey, author of *The 7 Habits of Highly Effective People*.

Think of the emotional trust account as you would a bank account. However, it's value is based on trust instead of money. Every time you interact with someone, they are making deposits of trust into or taking withdrawals out of your emotional trust account. To make a deposit, they say or do something that builds trust. To make a withdrawal, they say or do something that creates distrust.

Trust is a two-way street. While they are making deposits and withdrawals, so are you. When you're interacting with others, you are always making deposits or withdrawals, not only with them, but also with anyone who is watching.

Just as cash deposits and withdrawals can be large or

small, deposits of trust and withdrawals of distrust can be large or small. When someone no longer trusts the other person, the relationship is over. The emotional trust account is overdrawn.

Keep these terms in mind as you continue to read. When I use the term deposits and withdrawals throughout the rest of this book, they will be in reference to the emotional trust account.

When it comes to knowing your product or service, buyers are not typically impressed by your knowledge (competency). Buyers show up expecting the seller to know more about what they're selling than anyone else. That's logical. If I'm selling something, I should know everything about it. So, if you know everything about your product, you are not exceeding expectations. You are simply meeting expectations.

Let's consider knowledge of the product as it relates to the emotional trust account. If they expect you to know about the product and you do, you make a small deposit into their emotional trust account. If they expect you to know about the product and you don't, you make a big withdrawal. It's hard to make a big deposit, but it's easy to make a big withdrawal because all withdrawals tend to feel big.

Overall, deposits into the emotional trust account tend to be small, and withdrawals tend to be big. Since we expect deposits, when someone makes one, it's not that big of a deal. Since we expect deposits, when someone makes a withdrawal, it's always a big deal.

When it comes to knowledge about the product or service you're selling, you will answer every question and make deposits or provide some *"I don't knows"* and make some withdrawals. As my wife, Ria, wrote in her book *Leadership Gems,* *"Often, the little details are what will take you from mediocre to excellent and from average to exceptional."* When it comes to competency, *"little details"* mean you have all the answers, or you can get them quickly.

However, if you don't know the answer to a question, it's always best to say *"I don't know."* You may make a withdrawal, but you get some credit for being honest. But, pretending to know when you don't know sets you up for multiple withdrawals. At a minimum, one for not knowing and another for attempting to deceive the buyer. By the way, the principles of building trust apply at work and at home.

Trust is a big deal. With people, the little things are often the big things in terms of deposits and withdrawals. With trust, you accomplish great things. Without trust, you accomplish lesser things.

Invest your time, and your money if necessary, to develop your business: YOU. Whatever that means to you, do it. Why? Because YOU *will* always benefit. If your company will pay, that's a bonus. If they won't, don't let them cause your business to fail. YOU are responsible for the success of YOUR business.

I always recommend focusing 80% of your time on character development and 20% of your time on competency development. As the great Benjamin Franklin said, *"Empty the coins of your purse into your mind, and your mind will fill your purse with coins."* Development sells.

SELLER BEWARE

1. Character builds relationships, and competency delivers results. Rock stars excel in both areas!

2. You're either intentionally growing, or you're automatically slowing. Everything is changing!

3. If you won't invest in growing and developing yourself, why should anyone else? They shouldn't!

8

LEVERAGE YOUR CHARACTER

YOUR CHARACTER WILL EITHER
LAUNCH YOU OR LIMIT YOU

*"Character isn't something you were born with
and can't change, like your fingerprints.
It's something you weren't born with and must
take responsibility for forming." ~ Jim Rohn*

When I mention you need to develop your character, I'm not assuming you're a *"bad"* salesperson and need to become a *"good"* salesperson. Character is much more complex and dynamic than these two very simple and vague words.

Character cannot simply be defined as *"good"* or *"bad."* Every book I've ever written along with every leadership development and personal growth book I've ever read has been about character. There are many tens of thousands of them. If you truly want to learn about character, you must be prepared to go extremely deep and extremely wide. That's why I recommend 80% of your intentional growth be in the area of character.

I'm not trying to *"fix"* you because I don't think there's anything *"wrong"* with you. Since you're reading this book, my assumptions are you are *a person*, and you want to be *a better person*. I'm also assuming you want to increase your sales and improve your life.

When I say you need to grow and develop your character, I know you are a very unique and complex individual with all types of feelings and emotions. I also know those feelings and emotions guide you throughout your waking hours. They are behind the choices you do and don't make each day. All of this simply confirms one thing: you're human like the rest of us.

In the words of Margaret Jensen, *"Character is the sum total of all of our everyday choices."* This means who you are is determined by the choices you make. I've mentioned that if you want better results, you must change your mind. Changing your mind is a choice. Changing your character is a choice. Becoming a better salesperson is a choice.

When speaking about character, I always reference Henry Cloud's definition. He says, *"Character is the ability to meet the demands of reality."* A simple definition that isn't so simple. It covers it all, and there's a lot to cover.

If you can't meet the demands of reality, you have a character problem. This principle applies to us all.

If you're losing sales you should be making, you have a character problem. If you need more sales and can't figure out how to get them, you have a character problem. If you know how to get more sales but you won't actually do what you know you should do to get them, you have a character and an integrity problem.

Knowing what to do but not doing it is an integrity issue. I also prefer Cloud's definition of integrity. He says, *"Integrity is the courage to meet the demands of reality."* Therefore, to improve our character, we must increase our ability to do and/or develop the courage to do what we already know we should be doing. This may include something we should stop doing.

When it comes to leveraging your character to increase your sales and improve your *word of mouth*, it's not just about what you should start doing. Many salespeople are holding themselves back because of the things they won't stop doing. Saying *"No"* to the wrong things will give you space to say *"Yes"* to the right things. It says easy, but it does hard. One of my mentors, Les Brown, made this remark during one of my training sessions with him, *"In life, if you do what is easy your life will be hard. But, if you do what is hard, your life will be easy."* Do the hard things.

Here's an integrity challenge. It won't help me, but it *will* help you. That's my goal, but I can't do the work for you. If you're serious about *changing your mind* and improving your results, make a list right now. Don't wait.

On the list, write down ALL the things you already know you should stop doing. Things that waste your time, money, and energy. Things that in no way will improve your results. Social media, hobbies, beverages (don't forget the recovery time), socializing, playing games on your phone, sleeping more than needed, etc. It's okay if you don't plan to stop doing them. Just write them down, so you can see them all. When you're done, go back and estimate the time dedicated to each per week and the dollars dedicated to each per week.

It will cost nothing in terms of time or money to stop doing these things. What is preventing you from doing what you know you should do? It's a lack of integrity. Stop thinking about it. Just do it. Integrity sells.

SELLER BEWARE

1. Stop doing what you know you shouldn't be doing. This will free up more time to do the right things.
2. Keep doing what is working for you. If it's working, do more of it. What's stopping you?
3. Start doing what you know you should be doing. There's nothing stopping you but YOU!

9

WHAT'S YOUR MOTIVE?

YOUR INTENTION IS YOUR FIRST IMPRESSION

"There's no second chance to make a good first impression." ~ John C. Maxwell

Influence is the foundation of selling. However, until others trust us, we won't have any influence with them. Trust is the foundation of influence.

Trust is based on two components: character, *who we are*, is static and doesn't change from situation to situation; and competency, *what we know*, which is situational. We can be totally competent in one situation (selling a product) and totally incompetent in another situation (performing heart surgery) at the same time.

Consider the following example.

If you get to know me well enough, you may trust me unconditionally as a person based only upon my character. You may also trust my competency while teaching you principles of influence. However, trust in the area of competency is situational meaning it depends on how satisfied you are with my knowledge in your area of interest.

I may not know you personally, but I already know you would not trust me to do surgery on you. I'm not competent in that specific area. You would quickly realize it and would be able to verify it simply by asking me a few related questions. Every time a buyer is discussing your product or service, they are validating your competency. Depending on the buyer's satisfaction with your answers, you are either building trust or creating distrust.

Although you may trust me as a person, you would not trust me to do your surgery. I sold you on *me*, but I couldn't sell you on buying that specific service *from me*. Since trust is the foundation of influence, I would have no influence with you in that specific area regardless of my character.

Character + (the appropriate) Competency = Trust.

Knowing how character and competency collectively fit together is critical when considering the impact of trust on the seller/buyer relationship.

When it comes to sales, you're always selling two things: yourself (first) and the product or service (second). When you're selling yourself, the buyer will trust or distrust you based on your character. When you're selling your product or service, the buyer will trust or distrust you based on your character *and* your situational competency: who you are and what you know relative to the product or service.

If you can't sell yourself, the chances of selling a product or service are very low. If the buyer doesn't want to buy from you, they will fire you and look for another seller to hire.

Your character will determine how you approach and interact with the buyer. Your character will determine if you immediately begin to build trust or if you immediately begin to create distrust. By now, you should understand the impact of trust on your ability to sell yourself and your product or service. It's crucial. Have you considered what the foundation of trust is? Where does trust start?

Intention is the foundation of trust. Your intention

will either create the foundation for trust to be built into the relationship with the buyer, or it will ensure there is not a foundation upon which you can build trust. It's all about character. Who you are on the inside determines what the buyer will experience on the outside.

When it comes to selling yourself, your first impression with the buyer is based on how you initially make them feel. You can only influence that feeling, you can't determine it. How they feel is their choice.

If they feel your intention is to create a mutually beneficial relationship based on *their* best interests, your intention will result in your first deposit into the buyer's emotional trust account. However, if they feel your intention is simply to make the sale based only on *your* interests with no concern for *their* best interests, you just made your first withdrawal from their emotional trust account. You are instantly overdrawn…that's not good.

If you haven't made any deposits, but you chose to make a withdrawal, you're overdrawn from the very beginning of the relationship. That's not a strong selling position. That's definitely not how you want to start.

Unfortunately, you may be overdrawn before you meet them. How? There are many reasons such as: bad *word of mouth*, they don't trust salespeople, they had a bad experience last time, etc. The right intention sells.

SELLER BEWARE

1. *Your first impression is your first sale. Deposits get you hired. Withdrawals get you fired.*
2. *Character without competency is not enough. Competency without character is not enough.*
3. *The best salespeople make the most deposits. Deposits will make you. Withdrawals will break you.*

10

DON'T BE A SALESPUPPET

THE BEST SALESPEOPLE MOTIVATE; THE WORST SALESPEOPLE MANIPULATE

"Nice guys may appear to finish last, but usually they are running a different race." ~ Norman Vincent Peale

My only child, Eric, will have his 26th birthday in 2017. Eric has read many personal growth and leadership development books. He understands the principles of character-based influence much better than most 40 or 50 year old people I know. He is an extremely exceptional young man with an amazingly bright future.

Several years ago, after Eric had been working full-time with me from age 19-21, he decided to give sales a try. He accepted a sales position as a new car salesman. We discussed how he would quickly rise to the top of the sales board because of his big advantage in the area of influence. He had big plans to implement what I'm sharing with you on these pages.

As often happens, things didn't go according to plan. He soon found out he wouldn't be able to do things his way, which is also my way. He was rushed through an intense and well-structured sales training program to *"help"* him learn *how to sell*. Their approach was different than his approach which is not to *"sell,"* but rather *to influence people to want to buy from him and not his competition.*

Eric and I quickly realized he was being trained how to

manipulate the buyers from the minute they came on the lot until the minute they left. Everything was scripted for him. Eric wasn't trained to be a salesperson. He was trained to be a salespuppet.

If I show up with purchasing in mind and begin to feel and experience the script of a well-rehearsed salespuppet, I'll always be nice, but *I'll never be back.*

I do not want to interact with a salespuppet. I want to interact with a salesperson. Don't be a salespuppet. If you're expected to be a salespuppet, you are being manipulated. They are not training you to sell yourself. They are training you to sell their product or service their way and leaving YOU out of the equation.

If you remain in this situation, you're allowing them to hold you back. My friend and author of *The Transformative Leader*, Amir Ghannad remarked, *"Being intentional about discovering the hidden ways in which we sabotage ourselves empowers us to expose and eliminate these invisible culprits."* If you're struggling, are you choosing to follow a sales script? If so, find a place where you can be a salesperson, and you will excel *if* you apply what you're learning on these pages.

Note: I highly encourage in-depth training on the product or services you are selling. Knowing about what you're selling doesn't make you a salespuppet. My focus here is on "how" you sell.

Eric wasn't expected to build strong, impactful, trusting relationships with his potential customers. Far from it, he was expected to follow the script which most buyers instantly consider a withdrawal. The script wasn't designed to look like a script. *"Get good, so they won't know it's a script."* they say. However, intention is not something the buyer will see. *Intention is something the buyer will feel.*

Needless to say, Eric didn't do very well attempting to cast the *"sales"* spell which had been formulated by the sales wizards up above. Playing games with buyers doesn't motivate them to buy, it motivates them to fire the salesperson and hire another one at a better led company.

When a buyer meets a salesperson, they are most often expecting to be manipulated in some way. Why? Because it's common for many salespeople to go through the same type of manipulative training that Eric was put through. Of course, it wasn't called *"manipulation training."* It was glossed over and called *"sales training."*

During the short time he was there, he struggled and watched the revolving sales door swing open and closed as other salespeople came and went. They were set up to fail from the start. Of course, they had a rock star at the top of their sales leader board like every other team. In this case, it simply indicated who was willing to play the manipulation game and who was the best at it.

Eric eventually moved to a company better aligned with his values. He launched like a rocket to the top of the sales board with no prior experience or knowledge of their products. He knew how to sell himself and started doing that on day one.

When your intention is to motivate, you seek mutual benefit and create a foundation for building trust. When your intention is to manipulate, you only seek personal benefit which creates distrust. Distrust is not the foundation of influence. Motivation sells.

SELLER BEWARE

1. When you are trained to manipulate others in order to make the sale, you're being trained to be a salespuppet.
2. Salespeople intentionally build trust. Salespuppets automatically create distrust. Trust is a must!
3. Salespeople focus on motivating buyers. Salespuppets focus on manipulating buyers. Emotions sell!

11

EMOTIONS RULE

ACTIONS ARE BASED ON EMOTIONS

"When dealing with people, you are not dealing with creatures of logic. You are dealing with creatures of emotion." ~ Dale Carnegie

I'm sure you are fully aware of the impact emotions have on the buyer's decision to buy the product or service. But, I want you to consider the impact emotions have on determining if the buyer will buy-in to YOU.

John C. Maxwell was on the mark when he said, *"People are more willing to take action when you first move them with emotion."* This is absolutely true when it comes to selling yourself.

The buyer won't always remember what you say or what you do, but they will always remember how you make them feel. You can be sure these feelings, good or bad, will be passed on to others through *word of mouth*. If you're very good or very bad, there's a good chance their feelings will lead them to share their experience with their social media network. How you make them feel will determine if that *word of mouth* is positive or negative.

Whether we choose to use the word feelings or the word emotions, we're talking about the exact same thing. Our thoughts determine our feelings. *The buyer will never believe what you tell them; they will only believe the story they tell themselves about what they heard you say.* Think about that.

Don't believe me? Odds are you just finished doing it

31

and may even still be doing it at this very moment. You may even stop now and do it again to be sure. It's a human condition. It's what we do and how we're wired.

When you read my words, you most likely paused, read them again and asked yourself, *"Is what Mack stated true?"* Then, you told yourself a story of agreement or a story of disagreement. Either way, your belief in my words was based on your thoughts, not my words. Your emotions were also generated by your thoughts, not my words.

Think back on the previous pages, you've been doing it since you started reading my book. Your potential buyers will begin telling themselves stories about you the moment they hear the *word of mouth* about you or the moment they meet you. Their truth lies in their head and will be based on the emotions their story generates.

The story the buyer generates will be based upon their values, beliefs, and their experiences in the world. We see the world as we are, not as it is. This principle explains why multiple people can have the same experience but experience it differently. It's because they tell themselves completely different stories that generate completely different emotions.

This insight should provide a much better and deeper understanding of what is meant by, *"Perception is reality."* A person's perception may or may not be accurate. If your perception is in alignment with the true reality, then it is true. If your perception is not in alignment with the true reality, then it is false. A more accurate statement would be, *"Your perception determines your reality."*

Your emotions influence your choices. In my book, *Defining Influence: Increasing Your Influence Increases Your Options*, I dedicated six pages to *The Choice Formula*: *Thoughts + Emotions + Action = Choice.*

As you can see, thought is the foundation for choice. You already know you act on what you perceive to be reality.

When you fully understand your thoughts lead to your feelings and your feelings lead to your actions, you will become much more intentional and try to influence the buyer to have more positive thoughts.

How you choose to influence a buyer will be based on your character. You can choose to influence them for only your benefit, which is manipulation. Or, you can choose to influence them for mutual benefit, which is motivation.

If you choose manipulation as your motive, they will tell themselves a negative story and generate negative feelings about you. You are more likely to be fired and will receive *negative word of mouth*. If you choose motivation as your motive, they will tell themselves a positive story and generate positive feelings about you. You are more likely to be hired and will receive *positive word of mouth*.

SELLER BEWARE

1. *Your intention, motive, agenda, and behavior will stir the emotions that will either make you or break you.*
2. *Your perception of reality determines the story you will tell and the emotions you will feel. Feelings sell!*
3. *You can't change someone's perception. But, who you are will influence the story they tell themselves.*

12

THINK SHORT TERM

I WANT THEM TO BUY FROM ME

"Like leads to trust. Trust leads to buying.
Buying leads to relationship." ~ Jeffrey Gitomer

When it comes to selling, how you think about the short term will dramatically impact how successful you are in the long term. It's natural to focus on the sale today because it's happening now. It's right in front of you. The next sale from this buyer may or may not ever happen.

It's important to note, the same principles that will help you long term are the same principles that will help you sell yourself short term. If you learn and intentionally apply the principles I'm sharing, you will be on track for a great long term sales career filled with referrals, repeat customers, and lots of *positive word of mouth*.

Highly effective salespeople know a secret: The best chance to sell themselves, sell their product or service, get repeat business in the future, get referrals, and get *positive word of mouth* is to make a friend instead of making a sale. *The best salespeople always focus on making friends, not sales.*

Sure, that's common sense. But, it's not commonly practiced.

There are a lot of things people know they should do because it's common sense. I've discovered when people say something is common sense what they mean is everyone will understand they should do it. I've also learned many of the things in life that can be understood with common sense cannot be applied with common sense. Doing many of the things in life that are commonly understood often requires *uncommon sense*. In order to do the things you know you should do, you often must have a higher level of intellectual capacity.

Focus on making a friend instead of focusing on making the sale. It's easier to sell to a friend who trusts you than to sell to someone who distrusts you or questions your integrity. Common sense right? However, it takes uncommon sense to focus on building a friendship based on trust instead of simply trying to make a quick sale. You must choose to go slower.

If you focus only on what's best in the current moment, you may get the sale. But, you may miss the opportunity to establish a long term relationship. If you focus on the future, you may get the current sale while taking extra time to establish a lasting relationship. You can do both, but start by intentionally building trust.

I've got the perfect example to illustrate this lesson. Ria and I moved to the Atlanta, GA area in the summer of 2015. We brought most of our furniture along, but not our sofa and loveseat. We drove to Atlanta a few weeks in advance to buy a new set and to schedule the delivery for the day we were officially moving in, so we wouldn't have to store it or wait for it.

When we walked into the first furniture store, we were approached by a salesman. I don't like to be approached by a salesperson when I'm shopping, but I understand they are there to make a sale. So, I put on a smile, maintain my best character-based behavior, and live with it. I like to look and be left alone while I'm looking. No one knows what I want and need more than me. I'm always nice, but I don't like clingy salespeople who recommend things to me. If I want to buy something, they will be the first to know.

As he approached, the salesman greeted us, *"My name is Carl. How can I help you?"* I replied, *"Carl, we're looking for living room furniture. If you can simply point us in the right direction, that's all we need at the moment."* He said, *"It's that way sir."* and pointed us in the right direction.

I liked that! He didn't try to lead us to it as most amateur salespeople would have done. He was a real sales pro! We liked him immediately and knew we would most likely buy from him. *"Thanks Carl! I prefer to just look around. If I find something, you will be the first to know."* I said. *"Yes sir!"* he replied with a nod and a smile.

He didn't bother us again. We made our selection, found Carl, and told him what we wanted. What he did next sealed the deal. Carl said, *"You seem to really like this one. It's a great deal and the quality is great. I'm confident you will not find a better deal or better quality. Have you already been to any other stores?"* We replied, *"No sir. This is our first stop. We got lucky too!"*

Amateur salespeople would have started processing our payment, but not Carl. He offered the names of three competitors, directions to them, and a suggestion to go look around before making our purchase. I knew he was one of those very special salespeople who was focused on making friends instead of making sales.

We left the store, drove to the end of the street, turned around, went back, and bought from Carl. He wasn't just another salesperson. *He was our friend.* Friendship sells.

SELLER BEWARE

1. *You go farther faster simply by making friends.*
2. *Your character is revealed by your words and behavior.*
3. *When you blow them away with character, they buy!*

13

THINK LONG TERM

I WANT THEM TO BUY FROM ME AGAIN

"If I try to use human influence strategies and tactics of how to get other people to do what I want, to work better, to be more motivated, to like me and each other - while my character is fundamentally flawed, marked by duplicity or insincerity - then, in the long run, I cannot be successful. My duplicity will breed distrust, and everything I do - even using so-called good human relations techniques - will be perceived as manipulative." ~ Stephen R. Covey

Carl is a true sales pro who understands character-based influence. He's a motivator, not a manipulator. He's a living example of the principles I'm sharing. Carl was thinking about the long term relationship from the very start and wasn't going to change his long term strategy based on the potential of short term success.

Carl had secured the short term sale. However, he proceeded to leverage the opportunity to secure his future sales with us by making additional deposits into our emotional trust account by recommending we visit his competitors. Carl was authentically demonstrating he had our best interests in mind, not his own. That was a big deal. Imagine the positive story both of us told ourselves about Carl after that moment.

Carl had selfless character. Selfless character sells. It also leads to a lot of *positive word of mouth*. Even if you don't get the current sale, it provides you with the potential opportunity for many future sales with the potential buyer in front of you and the potential buyers who will hear good things about you. That's long term selling.

Carl had common sense. But, he also had a high degree of *uncommon sense* which was evident from the moment we met him. He focused on making deposits in order to build trust for the short term sale by listening to my every word and responding based on those words.

He pointed me in the right direction as I asked. He didn't lead me there. He understood I wanted to look around by myself without his assistance. He didn't bother us. He didn't hover nearby. He left us alone. All of this was very effective short term selling, but it's also very effective long term selling.

I'm sure Stephen R. Covey was thinking about intent when he said, *"Eventually, if there isn't deep integrity and fundamental character strength, the challenges of life will cause true motives to surface and human relationship failure will replace short-term success."* Carl made sure we understood he had deep integrity and strong character, with actions not words.

If Carl had led us to the living room section of the store, that would have been an instant withdrawal. You may be thinking, *"That would have been a nice thing for him to do."* Some sales managers would say, *"It's in the script. You stay with the customer. Be there to answer their questions and to sell the product. Show them you care. Don't just walk away."* In other words, follow the script like a good salespuppet and get good salespuppet results.

But, I didn't want him to *"stay with me."* Doing so would have shown me he didn't care. I clearly said I wanted him to leave us alone. I didn't ask him to lead us there. I wanted him to point us in the right direction. He actually listened which resulted in a deposit. If he had not listened, it would have resulted in a withdrawal. He also made another deposit by not bothering us.

When my friend, Steve Lynott, heard I was writing this book to help salespeople excel, he provided a few stories and permission to use them. One of them fits perfectly here to illustrate the true results of long term thinking when selling. Here's a short story about another sales pro:

"My dad, Matt Lynott, raised 8 kids as a straight commission salesman for 46 years.

Dad sold yearbooks and class rings to high schools in northern Pennsylvania from the late 1940's to the mid 1990's. His career outlasted the founder of the company. He sold to year book advisors, many of whom he became good friends with over the years. One advisor had been a client for over 30 years. Dad sold well into his 70's and competitors often used this against him: 'Matt's getting up there, he doesn't understand the new technology, his ideas are no longer fresh' were just a few of the jabs. This advisor listened to one of the young talented competitors and said, 'Son, I like your company, I like you, and I like your product. I want you to come back and see me when you see Matt Lynott's name in the obituaries.'"

SELLER BEWARE

1. Your best strategy for short term selling is long term thinking. All salespuppet scripts focus only on the short term.

2. You're better off to treat each buyer as an individual. Listen to them. There is no one size fits all script!

3. Don't sacrifice your long term success! Short term salespuppet scripts benefit the company most, not you.

14

AUTHENTICITY SELLS

AUTHENTICITY IS ABOUT BEING, NOT APPEARING TO BE

"Into the hands of every individual is given a marvelous power for good or evil - the silent, unconscious, unseen influence of his life. This is simply the constant radiation of what man really is, not what he pretends to be."
~ William George Jordan

My main focus so far has been to help you understand *why* character-based selling is important. It's important in selling yourself first, and short term sales, but it's also important in long term sales.

There are many important character traits that will help you become highly effective at building strong, long lasting buyer-focused relationships. I've chosen a few of those I believe to be most critical for establishing a meaningful buyer/seller relationship.

Keep in mind, the context of what I'm teaching is related to selling. However, because I am teaching you principles, they are applicable in all relationships, personal and professional. Most salespuppet scripts assume buyers are generally all the same. These scripts tend to be filled with what the sales department leader or another sales guru has determined to be the *"best"* practices.

Practices only work in specific situations. Principles work in all situations. If you learn principles, there's no need to learn practices. This book is packed full of principles for that exact reason. I don't waste time teaching practices because if the situation changes the practice will no longer be effective. Then what?

My friend and author of *Gratitude Marketing*, Michael F. Sciortino, Sr. shared these words on the topic of authenticity, *"There's simply no substitute for authentic, personal, human-to-human relationships."* The key word here is authentic.

The most common comment Ria and I receive after speaking is, *"You two are so authentic."* For us, that's the best compliment we can receive. We don't have to tell people, *"We're authentic so look for it in our speech."* We simply are authentic, and that allows the audience to see it, feel it, and experience it.

The alternative is to be fake. Following a salespuppet script oozes *"I'm being fake."* from the start because most often the established *"best"* practice is expected to be followed and is forced upon the buyer whether it fits into the conversation and situation or not. The buyer instantly feels the lack of authenticity in the seller. It screams to the buyer, *"I'm trying to take you somewhere I want you to go."*

That's pure manipulation which creates distrust. The buyer will feel it. Then, they will start telling themselves stories about you and your company. Keep it up, and they're most likely to make an authentic exit and provide authentic *negative word of mouth.*

Many salespeople are learning *how to appear to be* (fake) instead of learning *how to actually be* (authentic). Some sales leaders truly believe teaching their sales team how to be fake is better than teaching them how to be authentic. Poor sales and turnover at the bottom is most often a direct result of poor leadership at the top.

Don't let poor leadership stop you from selling

yourself authentically. It's your choice to be authentic or to be fake. Choose wisely.

You're a buyer too. Which type of salesperson do you prefer? Someone who is authentic? Or, someone who is not? We all want authentic relationships. It's common sense right? However, being authentic often requires uncommon sense, especially when the boss expects you to follow the script. Working for a boss who doesn't have your best interests in mind is also a choice. Just as customers can fire you, you can also fire your boss.

The most authentic salespeople always go out of their way to make the buyer feel valued as a person. They tend to want to make small talk and get to know the buyer. They allow the buyer to lead the conversation and the interaction. They're not preoccupied with moving the buyer to a certain place at a certain speed.

What I loved about Carl was he never tried to sell us anything. His focus was to influence us to *want* to buy from him. Based on what I've been teaching you, he was actually trying to sell us something the entire time: himself. Authentic salespeople focus on selling themselves because their intent is to truly build a relationship. Selling the product is a natural outcome when you're able to effectively sell yourself.

SELLER BEWARE

1. The moment the buyer feels you're not being authentic is the moment you begin to lose the sale. Be real!

2. Whenever you are being authentic, you are always making deposits with the buyer. Make more deposits!

3. Say no to salespuppet scripts that force you to be less than authentic. If you don't, you will pay the price.

15

TRUTH SELLS

DON'T TELL THEM WHAT THEY WANT TO HEAR; TELL THEM THE TRUTH

"The best thing about telling the truth is you never have to think about what to say." ~ Mark Twain

If your intention is to be authentic with the buyer, there's no better place to start than with the truth.

If you're new to sales, say, *"I'm new to sales."* But, don't stop there. Work to earn the buyer's trust by declaring your intention by adding, *"But, I'm not new to selling myself and building great relationships. My ultimate goal is to earn your trust, not to make the sale."* The buyer is much more concerned with doing business with an honest seller who values them as a person. If you build the relationship, the buyer will want to help you succeed in your new role.

If you're new to the company, say, *"I haven't been with this company long."* But, don't stop there. Work to earn their trust by declaring your intention by adding, *"But, I have a great support team and won't hesitate to reach out to them if I need help answering any of your questions. I'm not afraid to ask for help when I need it."* You've just assured the buyer you are humble and want to provide accurate information and don't plan to go it alone.

If the buyer asks for something you don't have or can't provide, say, *"Unfortunately, I can't help you."* But, don't stop there. Work to earn their trust by declaring your intention by adding, *"But, I may be able to refer you to someone in my network who can help you."* Offer to help them get what they actually want. Helping a buyer get what they actually want will build trust. You may not sell the product, but you will sell yourself. You may or may not get their business in the future, but you will get their *positive word of mouth* and potentially some referrals because the buyer knows your character.

If the buyer makes an offer you know you can't agree to, say, *"I'm sorry, I can't go that low."* But, don't stop there. Work to earn their trust by declaring your intention by adding, *"And, I don't want to waste your time pretending to negotiate when I know I can't get to where you want to be."*

My friend, mentor, and retired (33 years) President/COO of Chick-fil-A, Jimmy Collins says it this way, *"It is kindness to refuse immediately what you eventually intend to deny."* I think you will agree, kindness will always build trust. Dee Ann Turner, VP of Talent (30 years) at Chick-fil-A, added this thought, *"Refusing immediately what you eventually intend to deny will ensure your credibility and integrity remain intact."*

When you know the truth isn't going to help you make the current sale, always tell the truth. But, always be sure to make an additional deposit into the buyer's emotional trust account by adding to it with some supporting information that will help sell YOU. Doing so will help you with potential future sales.

Delaying or avoiding the truth creates distrust. Telling the truth builds trust. The truth strengthens all relationships. The truth demonstrates character. The truth helps convert short term encounters into long term relationships.

If you're not going to tell the truth, then you're choosing to tell a lie. Who wants to buy from a liar?

There's no watering down the truth. It's either the truth, or it's a lie. If it's in the gray area, it's a lie. If it's beating around the bush, it's a lie. The only thing that is the truth is the truth.

Salespeople who have a long term mindset are the same ones who have made speaking the truth a habit. Not sometimes, all the time. They know speaking the truth is not only about the current sale. They know speaking the truth is about many potential future sales. It's always better to risk losing the current sale with the truth than to risk losing many future sales with a lie.

Ria and I had a product installed at our home many years ago. During the buying process, the salesman was great. He was nice as could be. He was prompt returning our calls. But, as soon as the sale was complete, he turned into a different person. He wouldn't return our calls in a timely manner. There were many promises he didn't keep. And, worst of all, he lied to us about many things after the sale.

We loved the product, but we would *never* give him *positive word of mouth* and never refer him or his company. We were sold on him until after the sale. He is the perfect example of a short term thinking salesperson.

When it comes to telling the truth, Ria took it to a new level when she said, *"Transparency is the purest form of the truth."*

SELLER BEWARE
1. If you value the buyer, be truthful. Honesty reflects who you are and what you value.
2. The only thing worse than telling a lie to a buyer is trying to convince them it's the truth. Be honest!
3. If you're truly long term selling, you'll never stray from the truth. Only short term sellers are dishonest.

16

TRANSPARENCY SELLS

TRANSPARENCY IS TELLING THE TRUTH WHEN YOU DON'T HAVE TO SIMPLY BECAUSE YOU WANT TO

"Our work, our relationships, and our lives succeed or fail one conversation at a time." ~ Susan Scott

If you want to leverage the truth, you can make additional deposits by being transparent. How? Tell the truth when you don't have to simply because you want to. When you tell the truth when you don't have to, the buyer will trust you more not less.

Telling the truth to a buyer when you don't have to lets them know you have their best interests in mind. Only the most skilled salespeople leverage the principle of transparency. When it comes to truth telling, transparency is king.

Amateur salespeople, regardless of years of experience or title, would say, *"If they don't ask, you don't tell! Never reveal anything you don't have to."*

As Ralph Waldo Emerson remarked, *"What you are shouts so loudly in my ears I cannot hear what you say."* Your character is always shouting who you are to the buyer and everyone else. You can't hear it, but everyone else can.

Telling the truth shouts to buyers that you're honest when you're supposed to be. Being transparent shouts to buyers that you are choosing to be honest and open when you don't have to be. Transparency communicates you are on the buyer's team, sharing information you have simply because you know they would like to have it. Transparency allows you to make big deposits.

When I sell something, I ask the price I expect to get, not the price where I want to begin negotiations. I'm not into negotiating. I don't like haggling when I'm buying or when I'm selling. This is one of the first things I tell the buyer when I'm selling. This will save us both time. If the buyer must pay the full asking price, I'm not only being transparent by telling them up front, but I'm also being respectful.

Several years ago, I decided to sell my 2003 Corvette Z06. My wife Ria called it *"The Other Woman"* because I took such good care of it and spent so much time driving and cleaning it. It had 110,000 miles and was in excellent condition. It was still basically like brand new. I created an online ad with pictures and detailed information. I had no intention of negotiating my asking price.

Soon after listing it, I received a call from a potential buyer in Ohio, several states away from where I lived in Alabama. He was very interested since it was the 50th Anniversary year model. As a car enthusiast, he had lots of questions. They were all easy to answer because the car was truly in excellent condition.

After he had asked all of his questions and was satisfied with my answers, he said he would take it. *"That's great,"* I said, *"but in full transparency, there's a few things you need to know that you didn't ask about."* I proceeded to tell him it had a small tear on the driver's side seat and one of the air conditioning vents had been broken. I told him I had glued the vent back together before I decided to sell it, so he wouldn't be able to notice it. I also told him I had all of the original parts to go with the car.

I didn't have to tell him about those things. He didn't ask. I especially didn't have to tell him about the broken vent. I knew exactly what I was doing. First of all, I was being honest. Second of all, I was being transparent. Since I didn't have to tell him those things, it meant more because he had already decided to buy the car.

He knew I wasn't trying to manipulate him because I had his best interests in mind, not mine. He could have easily changed his mind. However, my intent was to build trust, and that's exactly what I did. He won, and I won.

He thanked me and mentioned how honest he thought I was. He mailed me a money order for the full asking price two weeks before he saw the car. His money was in my bank, and the car that was now his sat in my garage for two weeks before he arrived to pick it up. Because of my transparency, he trusted me. Trust sells.

SELLER BEWARE
1. Transparency is a deeper level of truth. Be transparent!
2. Transparency can be leveraged for extra deposits.
3. Your character will determine how transparent you are.

17

INTEGRITY SELLS

MAKE AND KEEP COMMITMENTS

"You can't build a reputation on what you are going to do." ~ Henry Ford

When it comes to making deposits and building trust, many amateur salespeople slip up in the area of making and keeping commitments. They tend to often over promise and under deliver. This is something every salesperson can control and influence. Yet, many make withdrawals with buyers that they shouldn't be making.

Integrity is a major component of character. Salespeople with little or no integrity may or may not get the short term sale. It depends on how far into the sale they are when their lack of integrity rises to the surface and what other character flaws may have been revealed.

Buyers have fired many salespeople in the past due to lack of integrity, and they will fire more in the future.

If the salesperson's lack of integrity is revealed early in the relationship, they will likely lose the short term sale. If it's later in the process, they may get the short term sale because the buyer simply doesn't want to start over with someone else or waste any more time on the purchase.

However, the odds of the buyer being a repeat customer, referring business, or providing *positive word of mouth* is extremely low. They may speak highly of the product, but they won't speak highly of their salesperson.

Integrity, simply put, is doing what you said you would do, how you said you would do it, when you said you would do it because you said you would do it. Samuel L. Parker had this to say about integrity, *"Why do you enter into any activity with anything but commitment to achieve your objective of that activity - not a desire to achieve your objective, but a commitment?"*

Salespeople with high integrity make and keep commitments. Because they place an extremely high value on keeping their word, they don't make commitments lightly. They make commitments based on intentional thought related to reality, their schedule, the difficulty of the task, etc. They don't simply say, *"Yes, I can make it happen."* just to satisfy the buyer. They only say yes when they know without a doubt they can and will make it happen.

Rock stars in the world of sales always have a high degree of integrity. I don't mean rock stars on a given team or in a given company. I mean the real rock stars at the top of the sales mountain in their industry.

You can't climb to the top of the sales mountain with base camp character. You must have top of the mountain character to reach and remain at the top of the sales mountain. A salesperson with base camp character will get some sales by *accident*. But, they won't climb to the top of the leader board by accident.

Not keeping commitments guarantees you are making withdrawals. However, not making commitments at all will also be a withdrawal. There's only one way to make deposits when it comes to commitments: make them and keep them. Anything less will result in a withdrawal. Why? Because anything less means you won't commit, or you have been dishonest.

If you make a commitment and don't keep it, you have

lied. It's that simple. Saying you will do something and not doing it is a lie. You can sugarcoat a lie until you can't see it, but at the core you will still find a lie. You can make 1,000 excuses for why you lied, but you have still lied. Make commitments, then keep them.

As an example, when a salesperson schedules an appointment with me at 10:00 am, I expect to be meeting with them at 10:00 am, not some time after 10:00 am. I've had a lot of appointments with all types of salespeople in all types of businesses in my life. It's been more common for them to be late (lie) than to be on time (truth).

If it's a first appointment, whether in person or by phone, and they're late, I fire them immediately or soon after. They've already told me all I need to know about their character. My time is my most valuable asset. The seller may not value my time, but I do. I only want to invest my time with sellers who value my time too.

Have I bought from sellers who didn't value my time?

Yes. There have been sellers who got an *accidental* sale because I didn't want to spend time finding another seller. I simply wanted to buy and move on. Or, they got the sale because they had a product that was hard to find, well priced, or close to my home.

They *accidentally* got the short term sale. But, there wasn't a chance of them getting any more of my business, getting a referral, or *positive word of mouth*. They never knew I wasn't happy or had an issue. I was making deposits to get good service while I was there. They also never knew I wouldn't be back. They *thought* everything went great.

SELLER BEWARE

1. A happy buyer may not really be happy with you.
2. Making or breaking commitments reveals character.
3. Missed commitments lead to missed sales.

18

GRATITUDE SELLS

GRATITUDE ALLOWS YOU TO DEMONSTRATE RESPECT AND TO SHOW APPRECIATION

"Your success is measured, not by what the world gives to you, but by what you give to the world."
~ C. A. Munn

I know the buyer often doesn't value or respect the salesperson's time and efforts. However, this book isn't about how to get the buyer to build trust with the salesperson. As I mentioned earlier, it's *"seller beware"* because the buyer has the advantage. It's the seller's responsibility to grow and nurture the relationship with the buyer.

Unfortunately for the seller, the buyer doesn't have to work hard to learn these character-based principles in order to buy. They must only have a desire to buy in order to get a seat at the table. But, you must learn to apply these principles if you want to boost your sales and build long term relationships with raving customers who will follow you from company to company, if necessary, simply because they want to buy from you regardless of the brand or products you're selling.

One of the best ways to respect the sales relationships you already have is by showing gratitude. Many salespeople fail to nurture their existing sales because they are short term thinking. It takes extra energy and effort to intentionally interact with your loyal network. However, the return on investment through *positive word of mouth* can be very significant.

Michael F. Sciortino, Sr. said this in regard to nurturing your customers, *"Remember, your clients already like you. If they didn't, they wouldn't be doing business with you. In their minds, you are someone they respect. Showing your gratitude for their business can only enhance your position."* Are you enhancing your business (your sales) by demonstrating respect while leveraging gratitude? If not, you're missing the opportunity to turn your customer base into a *positive word of mouth* marketing base.

Showing gratitude is often an overlooked character trait. It takes a higher level of character to demonstrate respect and to show gratitude. However, showing gratitude communicates to the buyer that you remember them, appreciate them, and value them.

With people, the little things are often the big things. When I worked in the corporate world, there was a time I needed to order labels for a label maker on a regular basis. I didn't care where the labels came from and often ordered them from different sources while shopping around for the best price.

When I first started ordering them, I searched online, found a supplier, and made my purchase. There was no salesperson involved. I would get online. Place my order. Receive my package. And, repeat when I needed more.

Once after ordering from a new supplier, I received the package, opened it, and found a pleasant surprise. There was a personalized note thanking me for giving them an opportunity to supply the labels. That was different and offered an unusual, but nice, human touch.

By injecting this rare and unnecessary human touch, they were leveraging their influence through the only touch point they had (the package) by demonstrating respect for me as a preferred buyer and showing me gratitude as a caring supplier.

They already had the short term sale but wanted to ensure they also received my repeat business. They were intentionally expressing gratitude and respecting my choice to purchase from them knowing there were many competitors I could have chosen. They didn't know I actually bought from various suppliers.

Normally, I would have thought, *"Nice touch!"* and continued to shop around. But, they over delivered on showing gratitude. They didn't stop at the personalized note. The package also had a package of regular M&Ms and a package of peanut M&Ms. They took gratitude to the next level. All my future orders had M&Ms too. I was hooked.

Remember, with people, the little things are often the big things. They instantly became my *only* supplier. Their gratitude by way of chocolate made me a raving customer. I referred everyone to them, became a repeat customer, and provided lots of *positive word of mouth*.

Purchasing labels isn't something you normally talk about with others. They found a way to get their customers to order more, refer more, and talk more.

SELLER BEWARE

1. Respecting a buyer is a choice, especially when they may not respect you. Respect creates deposits!

2. Gratitude says I respect and appreciate you. Gratitude reveals your character. Appreciation sells!

3. Gratitude and respect will help you sell yourself. Showing gratitude is a competitive advantage.

19

CONNECTION SELLS

CONNECTION LEVERAGES COMMUNICATION

"In order to communicate, we must be sure we are connecting. If we are connected, communication will be much easier and effective. If we are disconnected, it doesn't matter what we are communicating because the message isn't getting through." ~ Ria Story

Matt Lynott said it perfectly, *"Every sale is made up of a series of conversations."*

Conversations are critical when it comes to selling yourself. Conversations lead to building trust or creating distrust. If what the buyer hears you say aligns with what they see you do, you will build trust. If what the buyer hears you say doesn't align with what they see you do, you will create distrust.

Conversations can also allow you to connect on a much deeper emotional level with the buyer. Nearly everyone knows how to communicate. But, only a few have mastered the art of connecting. The key to connecting is intentional storytelling. This is so vital for selling yourself and making the sale that Ria created an entire coaching/mentoring program in this area. To learn more, visit TopStoryLeadership.com/StoryTeller.

Michael F. Sciortino, Sr. made a very insightful comment when he said, *"Never forget facts tell, but stories sell...Facts satisfy the analytical part of our brain, but it is stories that touch our hearts."* In other words, stories stir our emotions.

Teaching, telling, and recommending speaks to the buyer's conscious mind and shines the spotlight directly on you. This is how you effectively communicate information and your thoughts to them. The buyer's conscious mind listens to you suspiciously: *"Stop right there! You don't know me. Who do you think you are telling me what I need, why I need it, and whether or not I can afford it?"*

The buyer's conscious mind *will* raise red flags and put them in a defensive posture. You already know it's hard to sell to a buyer who is in a defensive state of mind.

However, storytelling speaks to the buyer's subconscious mind. This is how you effectively connect with them. The buyer's subconscious mind listens to you trustingly: *"I'm paying attention. This is actually interesting. I don't want to miss anything that may be important to me. I can relate. Is there something in this story that applies to me? If so, what does it mean to me? This is something I need to think about."*

The buyer's subconscious mind will tap them on the shoulder and ensure they're paying attention and are in a receptive posture. When the buyer is in a receptive posture, they are more open to your communication.

As the seller, you must tell the facts, but you should also become skilled at telling stories to support the facts.

Reflect on and consider what I have taught you so far. You may struggle a bit to come up with specifics. However, odds are good you can still easily remember and relate to the stories and the lessons in them such as me selling my Corvette, Carl recommending his competitors, and Matt Lynott's dedicated customer who advised the rookie to come back only after reading Matt's obituary.

Reflect on your own experiences in conferences and seminars. Were the best speakers (sellers) those telling stories or those simply sharing facts that were already listed on the PowerPoint or your handout? There's nothing wrong with sharing facts. You should share facts. But, make a habit of supporting them with stories.

If you don't know any good stories, ask other salespeople in your business, ask people who like and enjoy using the product or service you're selling, or try it out yourself if you haven't already. Sharing stories of your own positive experience and how you personally benefited will give you credibility and help you connect with the buyers at a deeper level.

If you're selling a product, go visit the manufacturing facility. Walk slowly through the entire process from start to finish. Talk to the people along the way, ask their names, and ask them lots of questions. Learn how they do what they do and why they do it, so you can tell stories about your visit and what happens inside the factory.

SELLER BEWARE

1. Always focus your energy on connecting before you start communicating. Storytelling sells!

2. Everyone communicates but few connect. Connecting goes beyond words and triggers emotions.

3. Storytelling makes you memorable. Storytelling causes others to tell stories about you. Tell more stories!

20

PRINCIPLES SELL

PRINCIPLES APPLY IN ALL SITUATIONS; PRACTICES APPLY IN SOME SITUATIONS

"Principles are not invented by us or by society; they are the laws of the universe that pertain to human relationships and human organizations.
They are part of the human condition, consciousness, and conscience. To the degree people recognize and live in harmony with such basic principles as fairness, equity, justice, integrity, honesty, and trust, they move toward either survival and stability on the one hand or disintegration and destruction on the other."
~ Stephen R. Covey

Each buyer is unique. Each salesperson is unique. Each relationship is unique. Each sales experience is unique.

Far too often, sales leaders make the mistake of training and developing their salespeople to apply a set of pre-determined general practices and to follow a set of pre-determined general procedures. The leaders don't want their sales team to think and adjust to the real situation on the fly. Or, they believe they can't. *"Follow the script,"* they say. *"This method has been tested and proven to be the most effective."*

These leaders want their sales team to get the buyer to comply with their script. The leaders simply want their salespeople to do what they believe will provide the best opportunity to make the sale. Many of these sales leaders are not bad people. They are simply ignorant and don't know what they don't know when it comes to character-based selling and long term relationship building.

Instead of teaching their salespeople *how to be*, the leaders teach them *what to do*. Having a leadership position in sales doesn't automatically mean the leader knows *how to be*. Often, it means they were previously the best salespuppets. Be careful who you learn from.

However, I also know some leaders train their team with practices and procedures with the intention of manipulating not only the buyers, but also their sales staff. They don't trust them to do what's right. They tell them what they believe is right and try to control them and ensure they do as they are told.

Remember my comparison between salespeople and salespuppets earlier? Ignorant or manipulative sales leaders want salespuppets on their sales team. High impact, character-based sales leaders want high impact, character-based salespeople on their sales team.

When you learn practices, you learn *what to do* in certain situations. When you learn principles, you learn *how to be* in every situation. Ralph Waldo Emerson made a great point relative to principles when he said, *"The man who grasps principles can successfully select his own methods. The man who tries methods, ignoring principles, is sure to have trouble."*

To translate Emerson's words into my own, *"Salespeople who grasp principles can successfully select their own practices. Salespeople who try practices, while ignoring principles, are sure to have trouble."* When you learn principles, there is no need to learn practices. Principles will take the place of practices at all times. This book is filled with principles. However, applying the right principles will also allow you to learn the right practices related to that specific situation.

This may be a bit confusing on the surface, so I'll explain it using one simple example from my previous story about Carl selling me the living room furniture.

The first principle Carl applied was, *"Seek first to understand."* That applies to every situation. Every buyer in every situation wants to be understood by the seller. In order to do this, Carl listened intentionally. When I first spoke to him, he understood I wanted him to *"point me in the right direction."* He let me know he understood by doing exactly that. As a result, he began our relationship by making a deposit.

If Carl had been following a scripted practice requiring him to, *"Greet the customer at the door and show them to their area of interest."* he would have made no effort to understand me. He would have led me to the area and started our relationship with a withdrawal.

However, if that was what I had wanted, he could have applied the principle of *"Seek first to understand."* and made a deposit by showing me to the area once he knew that's what I preferred. In this simple example, you can see how the principle would apply in both situations, but the practice would not. Focus on principles not practices or scripts made for salespuppets.

SELLER BEWARE

1. You must always seek to understand the buyer in order to make deposits. The sooner, the better!
2. The key to highly effective human influence is to learn and apply principles. Read leadership books!
3. Don't depend on others to grow and develop you. Become intentional. Grow and develop yourself.

21

RAPPORT SELLS

WHEN YOU VALUE THE CUSTOMER, THE CUSTOMER WILL VALUE YOU

"You can't make the other fellow feel important in your presence if you secretly feel that he is a nobody."
~ Les Giblin

Rapport is defined by Merriam-Webster as, *"a friendly, harmonious relationship; especially a relationship characterized by agreement, mutual understanding, or empathy that makes communication possible or easy."*

Empathy is defined by Merriam-Webster as, *"the action of understanding, being aware of, being sensitive to, and vicariously experiencing the feelings, thoughts, and experience of another of either the past or present without having the feelings, thoughts, and experience fully communicated in an objectively explicit manner."*

Rapport (pronounced rap-or) defined in the very simplest of terms means: *I am like you, so it's okay to like me.* Most often, salespeople who are trained on the *practice* of establishing rapport are taught to mimic others. They are often taught to mimic: how others walk (speed), how others talk (speed/volume), the words being used (slang/terms), the posture, the energy, etc. These are all practices, and there are many more. However, none of these are principles.

After the short chapter on the value of principles versus practices, you can see how trying to learn, master, and keep up with all of the practices related to establishing rapport can become a significant challenge. I'm simple. I'm also busy. I also have no desire or need to learn all these practices because I already know the underlying foundational principle of building rapport.

If you will authentically master the one principle I'm about to teach you, this will be all you ever need to know about building rapport. Reflect again on my simple definition of rapport: *I am like you, so it's okay to like me.* What principle will allow you to convey this simple message to every buyer every time?

Notice, I didn't ask which practice because practices will only work in certain situations, with certain people, at certain times. In other words, practices cannot be consistently highly effective because there are too many variables. The key to becoming a highly effective and consistent salesperson is to master as many principles related to character-based human influence as possible.

Think about the first half of the rapport definition, *"I am like you."* How can I connect with every buyer I meet at the foundational level? What must I convey to them? I know this: everyone cares deeply about themselves. Not some people. All people.

The principle for building rapport is to authentically and sincerely convey to the buyer *you are like them because you truly care about them* just as they truly care about themselves. Bruce Barton put it this way, *"No man can persuade people to do what he wants them to do, unless he genuinely likes people, and believes what he wants them to do is to their own advantage."*

You can't fake rapport because the buyer will feel it. You can apply all the practices of establishing rapport you can find, but if this underlying principle isn't applied authentically and sincerely, all of the practices will be deemed manipulative and ineffective. If the principle is applied authentically and sincerely, the buyer will also feel it, and they will tell themselves a story, *"It's okay to like you because you like me."* In this case, you won't need to apply the practices. However, if you do, they will be well received, highly effective, and allow you to leverage the underlying principle to increase your influence.

If you truly want to convey you care about your customers, consider these words from Tim Sanders, *"You don't help others because of who they are, and how they can repay you. You should help them because it gives you an opportunity to do something incredible with all that you've learned and all you've become."* When you authentically help buyers, it's not about helping yourself get a sale. It's about helping them get what they want.

Tim's words reveal another principle related to establishing rapport. Every buyer wants to be helped. If you convey you are there to help them, they will tell themselves a story, *"Since I want you to help me and you want to help me, it's okay for me to like you."*

However, this principle must be applied on top of the foundational principle of *caring for the buyer*. If the buyer feels you don't care, when you offer to help, your help will be *perceived* as manipulative. Human influence is very complex and dynamic. The more you learn about influence, the more you will learn *there is more to learn*.

SELLER BEWARE

1. *If you don't care about what's best for the buyer, your influence will be limited from the start. Caring sells!*
2. *Your values and character will determine if you're able to authentically and sincerely build rapport. Be more!*
3. *Saying you care matters. But, what matters most is this: Does the buyer truly feel you care? Feelings sell!*

22

HELPING SELLS

STOP SELLING; START HELPING

"Try not to become men of success.
Rather, become men of value." ~ Albert Einstein

When you get the sale, you become more successful. If this is your primary goal, you are focusing on selling and are selfishly considering only the short term sale. When you help the buyer get what they want, you become more valuable. If this is your primary goal, you are focusing on helping and are selflessly considering the long term relationship.

Consider the two scenarios above. Assume you have the opportunity to do business with one of the two salespeople described above. Which one would you choose? Which one would you refer your mom too? Which one do you believe would get the most *positive word of mouth*? Which one would have more sales over their lifetime? The salesperson focused on helping wins.

Samuel L. Parker remarked, *"How many opportunities have you missed because you were not aware of the possibilities that would occur if you applied a small amount of effort beyond what you normally do?"* The principles in this book are all common sense. However, you must have uncommon sense to intentionally apply them and reap the rewards doing so will provide.

How can you become more intentional about helping

others? What questions can you ask? How can you be of more help by intentionally developing yourself? What do you need to learn? How can you help in a unique way?

When my son, Eric, went to work at the new car dealer, he and I discussed how he could be unique and different. How he could help buyers intentionally. How he could stand out from the crowd as a salesman who could and would help his customers in unique ways that were uncommon in the car selling business.

If you remember, Eric didn't get to unleash his true potential because he was unexpectedly processed straight into salespuppet training with full and explicit expectations of selling *their way* on *their terms* at *all times*. He was told, *"Follow the script, and you will prosper young man."*

After hearing how he was trained, how he was expected to interact with the buyers, and how he couldn't inject his own values and beliefs into *their* scripted selling process while serving *his* customers, I lost all respect for the organization and those leading it. The leaders were master manipulators of their sales staff and their customers. The type that give the good guys and gals a bad name. The leaders were not focused on helping anyone. They were focused on using everyone internally and externally for their own personal success.

Before he knew it would be that way, Eric and I had developed a plan for him to help his buyers authentically and sincerely. When they came on the lot, he wouldn't pressure them in any way. Although I hadn't met Carl in the furniture store at that time, we had actually developed a plan for Eric to help his buyers much like Carl helped me and Ria: Be hands off and helpful beyond the norm.

One thing Eric planned to do was to help buyers find the exact car they wanted even if it wasn't available on his lot. If he didn't have what the buyer wanted, his plan was not to manipulate them into buying something he did have as some salespeople would do. Instead, his plan was to help them find exactly what they were looking for.

Eric planned to ask for their phone number and/or email, not to put in a database to be harassed later, but so he could contact them when he found what they were looking for. Sure, he would look at his sister dealerships in case he could make a transfer. But, if it wasn't there, he planned to look for it at any dealership or with any individual. He just wanted to help the buyer find what they wanted.

Eric was going to use his slow time or time off to do an online search and notify the buyer of the details and the locations where they could find exactly what they were searching for, even if it was with a competitor. He was thinking long term.

He knew the buyers would be blown away and tell everyone about him, give him referrals, and give him *positive word of mouth*. He also knew, whenever they needed another car or heard of someone else in the market for a new car, he would be the first person they thought of because he would have helped them far beyond what was generally expected.

They wouldn't have seen him as a salesperson, but rather a trusted friend who helped them when he didn't have to.

SELLER BEWARE

1. *Helping others when you don't have to helps you make deposits and grows your influence. Helping sells!*

2. *Helping others when they least expect it makes you stand out from the crowd. Look for ways to stand out!*

3. *You don't always remember the 2nd or 3rd person who helps, but you do always remember the 1st who helps.*

23

RELATIONSHIPS SELL

UNTIL YOU SELL YOURSELF, YOU CAN'T BUILD A RELATIONSHIP

"If you make a sale, you can earn a commission.
If you make a friend, you can earn a fortune.
This philosophy is rarely used in sales.
Those who employ it are the top performers and the
top paid salespeople. They build relationships."
~ Jeffrey Gitomer

When Eric and I developed the plan to help the buyers he met while selling cars, neither of us had read the quote above. However, the principle in the quote *"If you make a friend, you can earn a fortune."* is the very principle he planned to apply along with many others. Eric didn't plan to chase commissions. He planned to make friends.

Making friends of buyers is a hard thing to do when you're expected to force your buyers into the sales funnel using a sales script.

I shared a story about my friend Steve Lynott's father, Matt, in an earlier chapter. Steve is very proud of the character and integrity his father displayed during his nearly 50 years as a very successful sales professional. Steve provided a second story that shines light on what relationship building looked like in his father's career.

Steve tells this story about his father, *"Near the latter stages of Dad's career, he took me with him as he made calls on his yearbook advisors. He wanted me to learn the business and see if it was something I was interested in pursuing. Dad and I entered one of the high schools he had been selling to for a long time. As we entered the year book advisor's office, the woman looked at me and said, 'You're Steve aren't you?' I was more than surprised. I had never met this woman before. She saw the startled look on my face. She reached down, opened her top drawer, and pulled out a picture of my entire family saying, 'I've known Matt for years and each one of you indirectly.'"*

Steve went on to say, *"I have been very troubled over the years at how people view sales professionals. They are seen as money hungry and not to be trusted. My father was a true professional. He loved his work and his clients, and they loved him back."*

If Steve's dad were alive today, he would be proud to know Steve is still sharing his stories. I'm also sure Matt could have done a much better job filling this book with principles and stories than me. I'm grateful Steve shared a little about his dad. It's a privilege to include a little about Matt's legacy on these pages. Matt's legacy is helping you make your greatest sale: yourself.

Do your repeat customers have a picture of your family? Would you even feel comfortable showing them one or giving them one? Do you discuss your personal life and your family with your customers? Do you know the name of their spouse or if they even have one? Do you know anything about their children or if they have any or want any?

Are you truly interested in anything other than making the next sale? I hope you are. If not, the question you must ask yourself is, *"What am I leaving on the table?"* And maybe more importantly, *"What does this say about my character? Do I truly care about my customers as people? Or, do I simply treat them as objects making purchases? What do my actions communicate to them about me?"*

As David Schwartz said, *"Big people monopolize the*

listening. Small people monopolize the talking." As I'm sure you know, salespeople love to talk. However, you may not know the very best salespeople would rather listen first and talk second. Sure, they love to talk too, but only after they have listened and feel they understand.

Most of the time when a true sales pro is talking, they are asking thought provoking or information gathering questions. This allows them to leverage their words to gain additional influence and to make a stronger and better connection with the buyer.

If salespeople are focused on making friends and building relationships, they want to learn more about the buyer, not what they want, how many they want, when they want it, or when they can pay for it. Amateurs tell others about their products. Professionals ask others about their lives.

Rob Waldman said it simply enough, "*Relationships are about relating. If you don't spend time relating...there won't be any relationship.*" Based on my own experience, many salespeople, who are focused on the short term sale, pack their schedule as full as they can get it. These same salespeople tend to also be those who are often late because they were with another customer. They also tend to rush their time with you because they know they have another appointment immediately when they're done with you. Think of your doctor or dentist. Are they relating?

SELLER BEWARE
1. *The stronger the relationship, the more sales you will have. Relationship sells!*
2. *The best salespeople build strong relationships. Their customers become their sales and marketing team.*
3. *Being late doesn't strengthen relationships. Rushing buyers doesn't strengthen relationships. Slow down!*

24

UNDERSTANDING SELLS

SQUINT WITH YOUR EARS;
LISTEN WITH YOUR EYES

*"How do we learn? 89% with our eyes, what we see.
10% with our ears, what we hear. The other 1%
of learning comes from the other senses."*
~ John C. Maxwell

Doctors and dentists are salespeople too. If you want to hear the *word of mouth* they are getting, sit in the waiting room for about 10 minutes. You'll hear plenty. If wait times are short, you'll hear *positive word of mouth*. If wait times are long, you'll hear *negative word of mouth*. Are they listening?

Some doctors and dentists understand the value of building strong relationships and value their customer's time. Those offices are well managed and well led. However, they are also booked solid and don't have any appointments for months. They get more referrals than they can process into their system. Their *word of mouth* is also positive. They are sales pros. Understanding sells.

When you're interacting with a buyer, listen with your eyes if you truly want to seek to understand them and help them feel understood. Often, they won't tell you what they're thinking. But, they will show you what they're feeling which is much more important since feelings and emotions drive behavior.

I've seen salespeople totally crash and burn in the area

of understanding. Often, they don't have an interest in understanding the buyer at all. Amateur salespeople focus on being understood by the buyer. These amateurs think the key to selling is to get the buyer to understand them.

Until the buyer feels understood, they have zero interest in listening to the salesperson. If I don't think you understand my needs, why would I want to listen to your solution or buy your product or service? You can't provide a solution if you don't understand the problem.

Several years back, I received a message from a friend. He wanted me to get on a call with him. He had started selling various types of health supplements and knew I was into fitness, so he thought I might have an interest. He planned a conference call with me and his sales pro mentor. The *"pro"* was actually going to do the selling since my friend was new to the program. My friend's mission: listen and learn (the script).

My friend obviously knew me, but the person who was going to show him how to sell was a stranger to me. Once we were all connected, my friend handed the conversation off to the *"pro."* The *"pro"* immediately began selling.

His first attempt was a total flop. He started with his script immediately. Somehow, never having met me and without asking me any questions, he thought I needed his amazing weight loss product, and he was going to sell it to me.

Since he wouldn't take a breath and I didn't want to be rude, I just let him go on and on and on. I was halfway through a 10 hour drive, so I had time. *"Follow the script, and you will be a success."* was ringing in my ears as I listened and listened. This *"pro"* wasn't the Energizer Bunny. He was the Energizer Salespuppet.

After about 30 minutes, he finally ran out of sales

script and asked, *"What do you think? Are you interested? It'll really help you lose weight."* My first comments to him while he caught his breath were, *"Well sir, I actually race mountain bikes, the kind you pedal. I ride and race nearly 3,000 miles off-road each year. I weigh less than 155 lbs. I think I'll pass."*

As any highly trained salespuppet would do, he didn't skip a beat or waste a moment seeking to understand. He jumped straight to the script for the next product he knew I needed. This time I got to listen for 30 minutes about an energy supplement that would be a healthy replacement for the coffee I drink in the morning and would give me energy all day long.

Then finally, he ran out of script again saying, *"What do you think? Are you interested? It's better for you than coffee?"* I replied, *"That sounds great, but I don't drink coffee, and I have more energy than I know what to do with. I actually need something to slow me down at times. I appreciate your time sir, but I'm out of time."* Then, I ended the call.

He obviously couldn't listen with his eyes since we were on a call. If so, he would have known I didn't need a weight loss product. If he could have seen me, hopefully he would have noticed I actually had something to say during his 30 minute script sessions.

He had some great products that I may have been interested in, but he never told me about those. I bought some later from someone else who asked me a few questions before they started selling.

SELLER BEWARE

1. Seeking first to understand will position you to sell. Understanding sells!
2. Focus on the buyer. Focus on their needs.
3. Understand the buyer's problem, so you can provide a solution. Problem solving sells!

25

SUPPORTING SELLS

WHEN YOU'RE THERE FOR YOUR CUSTOMER, THEY'LL BE THERE FOR YOU

"Service makes people feel honored, respected, and special." ~ Dee Ann Turner

I often hear people say, *"Everyone in the company is selling."* I agree. Several years ago, I was conducting a cross-functional leadership development program for all the employees of a 1,200 person company.

There were usually 20 or so people in each week long class which was mixed with all types of employees, from all types of areas, in all types of positions. There might be a VP sitting next to a fork lift driver, who was sitting next to an engineer, who was sitting next to a welder, who was sitting next to a salesperson from the other side of the country, who was sitting next to a receptionist.

The leaders of that company brought in their outside salespeople from all around the country and included them in the leadership development program. Most often, the salespeople aren't included in this type of development. Including them was the right thing to do. Many fantastic and beneficial relationships were created. The salespeople also went back into the field with some great stories to tell the customers.

I always made sure each class understood the salespeople were out in the field working hard to make a living and feed their families just like everyone else, even though they weren't often seen at the facility. I also reminded them how salespeople carry the extra burden and responsibility of selling enough product to ensure all 1,200 families were taken care of and fed. In other words, the salespeople had to sell enough to keep all 1,200 employees working, not just themselves.

Most team members in the room had never thought of it that way. This perspective really helped bring them all together as a team. Then, I asked everyone if they remembered seeing some of the salespeople bringing customers and potential customers through the manufacturing facility on tours.

I told them, *"Once the salespeople bring the customers through the door, they are no longer selling. They were simply touring them around the facility."* Then, I would ask, *"If the salespeople aren't selling, who is?"* Usually, someone sharp would quickly say, *"We are!"* Then, I let it sink in for a minute. I wanted to be sure they fully understood they were all selling.

Not only is everyone selling, everyone is in customer service too. At a minimum, you're serving other internal customers, your co-workers, throughout the organization. A common word used to describe this type of support and service is: teamwork. If you truly understand the first thing you must sell is yourself, then you will easily understand you're also in customer service.

Ultimately, you're there to serve your customer. Caring is serving. Helping is serving. Supporting is serving. Customer service is serving. Selling is serving.

Few have stated it as well as Napoleon Hill when he wrote, *"It is the practice of the majority of men to perform no more service than they feel they are being paid to perform. Fully 80% of all whom I have analyzed were suffering on account of this great mistake. You need have no fear of competition from the man who* says, 'I'm not paid to do that, therefore I'll not do it.' He will never be a dangerous competitor for your job." How true that is.

If you're going to successfully and effectively sell yourself, *everything* is your job. Why? Because if the customer expects you to do it and you don't do it or get it done, you have just made a withdrawal. It doesn't matter if it's your job or not because the customer doesn't care.

They are simply looking for someone to offer support when they need it. They don't want to hear someone start whining; they want to see someone start shining. When it's time to make something happen, you can step up or step aside. The buyer won't hesitate to find another salesperson who is willing to make things happen.

Amateur salespeople who don't yet realize they're working for themselves will dodge the responsibility for solving problems, developing solutions, and finding an answer. But, the sales pro who understands they are working for themselves will quickly, energetically, and positively step up to the plate and make things happen.

A sales pro will always help their team succeed because they know they are making deposits and/or withdrawals with everyone they interact with and everyone who is watching. This includes everyone above them, beside them, and below them.

As Peyton Manning said best, *"The most valuable players are those who make the most players valuable."*

SELLER BEWARE
1. Everyone is in the customer service business. Customer service sells!
2. Always be looking for someone to serve and support.
3. Every customer is your customer whether they're buying from you or someone else. Support sells!

26

ATTITUDE SELLS

DON'T WHINE...SHINE!

"Refuse to complain. Complaining is just a way of not taking responsibility, justifying doing nothing, and programming yourself to fail. Complaining creates the illusion that you have done something."
~ Les Brown

W. Clement Stone made the following observation, *"There is a little difference in people, but that little difference makes a big difference. The little difference is attitude. The big difference is whether it is positive or negative."* Just as shiny objects get noticed, so do shiny salespeople. Stay positive.

I've made many purchases over the years, and I've encountered salespeople with positive attitudes and negative attitudes. I've chosen to do an overwhelming majority of my business with those with a positive attitude. How important is attitude in sales? It's HUGE!

Imagine you have the opportunity to buy the same product from two salespeople. They have the same exact product at the same exact price. They are both amazing salespeople. You can't tell the difference between them except for one thing. One has a great attitude about everything. The other has a bad attitude and moans, groans, and whines about everything and everybody.

Which salesperson would you choose to do business with? Unless you have a bad attitude yourself and prefer to be around negative people, you will obviously pick the one with a positive attitude. It's very easy to see the impact attitude has on your influence when you clear away the other character traits and look at attitude alone.

You have the power and the freedom to choose your response during, and in spite of, any situation or circumstances. No one can take this freedom and ability away from you. Because you are response-able, you are therefore responsible.

It's your responsibility to choose your response in every situation. You cannot transfer this responsibility to anyone else. What this means is you, not someone else, are responsible for your attitude. Not the boss. Not the weather. Not the last buyer. Not the next buyer.

Amateur salespeople are sometimes positive toward the buyer but make the mistake of being negative toward members of their own team or their own company. The reason I refer to them as amateurs is because true sales pros are always positive toward everyone.

Salespeople who badmouth others, no matter who those others are, are creating distrust and making withdrawals with anyone who hears them. Bad attitudes are like open windows allowing the buyer to peer into the character of the salesperson. Who you are sometimes, matters all the time.

Often during the sales process, things don't go as planned. I'm sure you are well aware of that. When things don't go as planned, that's the perfect opportunity to leverage a positive attitude by shining, instead of whining. I'm reminded of the words of Bob Butera, *"What distinguishes winners from losers is that winners concentrate at all times on what they can do, not what they can't do."* This doesn't mean you pretend the problem doesn't exist. But, it does mean you choose to have a positive attitude with the buyer regardless of what is or isn't going right.

Attitude is a choice. The only person who can change your attitude is you.

Sales guru Jeffrey Gitomer said this about attitude, *"Attitude allows you to see the possibilities when opportunity strikes — because it often shows up in the form of adversity."* Jeffrey is telling you to leverage your attitude during adversity. Instead of getting bent out of shape and making withdrawals with the buyer and the members of your support team when things aren't going your way, be mentally strong.

Find a way to make deposits. Find a way to be positive when others are being negative and when others expect you to be negative. Often, your attitude will influence the buyer's attitude.

I've witnessed buyers get upset only because the seller was upset. Your attitude is contagious. You have 100% control and influence over yourself. You may not be able to prevent someone else's bad attitude, but you can prevent your own.

When it comes to character-based relationships and building trust, you must make deposits and consistently get things right. It only takes falling short in one area to make a withdrawal.

SELLER BEWARE

1. Whiners make withdrawals. Shiners make deposits.
2. Your attitude will make you or break you. Attitude sells!
3. Your attitude before and during the sale may be the determining factor related to you getting the sale.

27

RESPONSIBILITY SELLS

LOSERS FIND AN EXCUSE;
WINNERS FIND A WAY

"Solving complex problems requires an inquiring mind and the willingness to experiment one's way to a fresh solution." ~ Daniel Pink

For some, sales come easy. They simply show up, stand at a counter, and people come in and buy, hour after hour. Think of someone working at a fast-food restaurant, an automotive parts store, or a grocery store checkout line.

For others, they're in the right place at the right time. If I want a specific product, and it's sold close to my house, there's a good chance I'll shop close to home. If I want a product that's hard to find, when I do find it, I am very likely to buy it. If my purchasing decisions are based on lowest price, I will compare prices at various locations and buy where the price is the lowest. The salesperson will accidentally get the sale, but the location, availability, or price caused the sale.

Relative to selling, I classify these sales as incidental and accidental sales. The salesperson's character and competency play a very minor role in how, or if, the sale takes place. Their main contribution was in taking the order and processing the payment.

Much farther up the selling scale is intentional selling. This is where the salesperson has full responsibility for making the sale happen. Who they are and what they know will determine if they are able to make the sale. It won't just happen. There is obviously a wide gap of different scenarios between incidental or accidental selling and intentional selling.

Successful intentional selling requires salespeople to accept varying degrees of responsibility. The tougher it is to make the sale, the more responsibility the salesperson must accept to be successful.

In the *"seller beware"* age of Google, Siri, and the smartphone, it's more challenging than ever for sales people to influence customers before the decision point.

The interactions salespeople have with potential customers who are *"just shopping around"* have decreased, and often customers have made a purchasing decision before they meet the salesperson.

The best salespeople don't make excuses for this reality. These are factors they cannot control. They don't waste any time or energy worrying about factors they cannot influence. What the best salespeople do is accept responsibility for the factors they can control and work to improve them. They do what they do best: they find a way to make something happen.

Ria shared an example from her days of waiting tables in a steakhouse many years ago. Since tips are often based on a percentage of the customer's bill, larger bills often equal larger tips. However, the server risks making a withdrawal when trying to sell the guest something they don't want.

Ria said, *"Most often, when customers would come in to have a steak dinner, they already knew what cut they wanted. If they didn't want to spend much money, I wasn't going to be able to change their minds to believe that a filet was a better choice than the sirloin. The best servers understood that and didn't worry about it. The* *customer's decision was already made, so there was no reason to try and change their mind. What the best servers realized, is they could influence the add-ons. Maybe the customer planned to order their usual sirloin, but I could remind them how tasty it would be to top their sirloin with grilled shrimp for an extra $4.99. Or, maybe I shared how decadent the chocolate cake was because I had a slice last week and knew they would enjoy it. The best servers took time to understand what the customer wanted, and took responsibility for enhancing their experience, rather than making the bill bigger."*

Ria understood trying to upsell would be a withdrawal. But, she also understood enhancing the guests experience would be a deposit. She focused on the area where she had influence and avoided the areas she didn't.

As Les Brown noted, *"Complainers focus on what has happened and give up their power. Winners focus on making things happen and using their power to find solutions to their challenges."* Taking responsibility means choosing not to complain. Has complaining ever helped? No. Will it ever help? No. Has it ever hurt? Yes, because complaining reveals weak character. The more you complain, the less you obtain.

Taking responsibility without complaining leads to deposits. Dodging responsibility and complaining leads to withdrawals. Everything rises and falls on influence.

SELLER BEWARE

1. When you take responsibility for everything, you can change anything. Accept more responsibility!
2. Your first responsibility is to grow and develop yourself. The faster you grow, the more you'll know.
3. The more you grow, the farther you'll go. Growth sells!

28

NETWORKING SELLS

NETWORKING IS ABOUT SELLING YOURSELF, NOT YOUR PRODUCTS AND SERVICES

"You are a human magnet and you are constantly attracting to you people whose character harmonizes with your own." ~ Napoleon Hill

Do not make the amateur mistake of networking to sell your products or services. Do what the sales pros do. Network with the intention of selling yourself.

Networking should be about building relationships based on who you are, your character. Who you are is who you will attract. As you work to continuously grow and develop your character, the caliber and type of people you attract will change for the better.

Amateur salespeople do very little, if any, intentional networking. And when they do, they tend to immediately begin telling everyone they meet about *their* business and *their* product or services. Amateur salespeople are focused on the short term sell which is why they are so anxious to talk about *their* products and services.

Sales pros do a lot of intentional networking. If they're not selling, they're networking. When they're networking, they're not selling products. They are selling themselves and creating long term relationships. They understand the potential opportunity for receiving *positive word of mouth* from all those they meet while networking, if they're willing to set their products and services aside. They know there will be a time and place for that later.

If people want to know about your products and services, they will ask. Even then, if you're in networking mode, keep it light. Potential buyers in a networking interaction aren't usually asking because they want to hear your complete sales pitch and product list. They're simply curious about who you are and what you do. Or sometimes, they are just being nice.

Even if a buyer wants to hear your full pitch, don't fall into the short term trap. If you're truly focused on intentionally networking, simply make an appointment and do the selling of your products and services later when the location is better and private. If you are in the room to network (sell yourself), don't start selling your products and services. Stay the course. If you don't, you will miss the opportunity to connect with many others. Think long term while networking.

I've known many salespeople during my life. Some of them do very well because when they're not working they are intentionally networking. Some don't do very well. I've noticed those who aren't doing very well aren't doing much intentional networking. They tend to see selling as a job, and a job to them is from *"9am to 5pm, five days a week"* so to speak. The best salespeople know they are selling themselves, and they do it all day every day. They are always open for business.

There's a big gap between the principles used by the best salespeople and the practices used by the worst. There's also a big difference in their income.

When you're successful at selling yourself while networking, you're paid in referrals. If you're not getting enough referrals, maybe it's time to look at *how often* and *how* you are networking. Michael F. Sciortino, Sr. shared this fitting comment, *"Referrals are appreciation of a job well done."* When you network well, you will be referred often.

When you ask other people questions, you are allowing them to influence you. You can find out exactly what you need to know with a perfectly structured question. Asking questions also demonstrates a sincere interest in the other person. Asking questions is another way of making deposits, if you're listening to understand, instead of listening for a space to jump in. Listening sells.

One of the greatest networking questions you can ask is, *"Who do you know that I should know?"* Don't ask this question early on. Ask it later in the conversation. However, don't ask it as the conversation is wrapping up because the person you're talking to won't have enough time to fully answer. Be intentional with your questions.

Networking is about intentionally applying all the principles I've shared with you on these pages. I highly recommend reading this book again with networking in mind. Odds are, you first read it with selling in mind. But remember, this book is about selling yourself first which is also exactly what your goal is when you're networking.

Go back through it at least once, many times if you're truly serious about getting to the next level. However, the key is to get busy applying. As you read it again, be sure to mark it up, fold the pages, create a *"to apply"* action item list, and use it as a tool to move yourself forward. Then, read it again and repeat several months later.

SELLER BEWARE

1. If your calendar doesn't have specific dates for intentional networking, you're missing out.
2. If your competition is intentionally networking and you're not, some of your sales will become their sales.
3. Unless you're willing to pay the price of intentional networking, you will be passed up by those who are.

29

WHAT IF THEY DON'T BUY?

DON'T FORGET:
YOU'LL STILL BE SELLING TOMORROW

"How an individual plays the game shows part of his character. How he loses shows all of it."
~ John C. Maxwell

Few situations give you the opportunity to truly convey who you are on the inside like losing a sale does. The best in sales choose to shine. The worst in sales choose to whine. I learned something a long time ago that is fitting here, *"If the truth hurts, it probably should."*

Reflect on the quote above from John C. Maxwell. There is powerful meaning in his words. Until you lose the sale, the buyer doesn't really know who you are. If you choose to whine to them, other buyers, team members, friends, and family, everyone gets to look inside you and see who you really are, not who you pretend to be when things are going well.

Ria often says, *"When you squeeze a lemon, you get lemon juice."* Relative to selling, I say, *"When you squeeze a salesperson with poor character, you get whining. When you squeeze a salesperson with strong character, you get shining."* Shining sells!

I'm sure you never whine. But, if you know salespeople who do, share the following with them. Whining and complaining will only paint a negative picture of you for others to see. Don't do it. Whining does not help you sell yourself. Don't do it. Whining won't increase your *positive word of mouth*. Don't do it. Whining won't win a potential buyer over. Don't do it. Whining never helps. Don't do it.

Whining does not convey to the buyer or to anyone else listening that you truly had the buyer's best interests in mind. When you have the buyer's best interests in mind, you don't want to sell them something they don't want. When you have the buyer's best interests in mind, you don't want them to pay more than they can afford. When you have the buyer's best interests in mind, you support their decision not to buy.

G. K. Chesterton made a great point, *"How we think when we lose determines how long it will be before we win."* What a great example of long term thinking. If you get frustrated, you will make withdrawals, not only in your professional life, but also potentially in your personal life.

When you have the buyer's best interests in mind, they will also have your best interests in mind. Losing the short term sale gracefully ensures you do not lose the long term sale. You can lose the sale of the product or service without losing the most important sale: yourself.

The long term sale is about the buyer's next purchase. The long term sale is about ensuring the buyer chooses to provide *positive word of mouth* long after you lost the short term sale. How you lose determines the *word of mouth* you get, not only from the buyer, but from everyone watching.

The significance of *how* you sell yourself when you're losing the sale of the product or service must not be overlooked. Even when you're losing the sale, you still must keep selling yourself. As George Halas said so well, *"Nobody who ever gave his best regretted it."* Who you are on the inside is what others experience on the outside.

Every interaction with a buyer must be intentional.

Whether winning the sale or losing the sale, you must remain focused on making deposits into the buyer's emotional trust account. The relationship depends on your ability to do so.

Find a way to make intentional deposits when you lose a sale. You're responsible for maintaining the relationship. You can influence the feelings they have about you when they walk away. You can influence what they will or won't say on social media about you. Don't lose *more* sales simply because you lost *a* sale. Losing and winning is about much more than the sale. It's about YOU!

Often, when you've given up all hope of making the sale and have settled for making deposits instead, you may actually win the sale.

When you lose a sale, you often gain an opportunity. If you're positive and seek to fully understand why you lost the sale, you may find yourself winning the sale at the very last moment. Why? Understanding sells! Connection sells! Deposits sell!

If you are truly *"seeking to understand,"* it won't always work. But, it might work. You don't do it because it might work. That's not authentic. You do it because it's the right thing to do whether you're winning or losing. That is being authentic. Authenticity sells!

If you apply everything you've learned in this book, you will get more sales and lose less sales. Sell yourself!

SELLER BEWARE

1. Don't stop selling because you lost the sale. You must continue to sell yourself after losing the sale.
2. You decide how you will lose. Therefore, you also determine how long it will be before you win again.
3. Every time you lose a sale you have the opportunity to make it a win. To do so, shine don't whine!

30

SOLD!

NOW, IT'S TIME TO OVER DELIVER

"I don't believe there is a thing of principle in connection with this success philosophy that will get an individual ahead so far and so fast and so definitely as the habit of going the extra mile; that is, doing something useful for other people and forgetting for the time being about what you're going to get back in return. Going the extra mile means that you render more service and better service than you're paid to render, but you do it all the time and in a fine, friendly spirit." ~ Napoleon Hill

I often ask salespeople if they over deliver. Nearly all of them respond instantly, *"All the time!"* However, when I get specific and say, *"Tell me how you over delivered with your last customer and the two before that."* they usually get quiet.

If they get quiet, I know they aren't truly over delivering. How do I know? They have nothing to instantly say. They've got to think about it. I've had this conversation enough to know those who are over delivering do so intentionally. They can provide details quickly because they have made a habit of going above and beyond what's expected.

Do you over deliver? If so, how? If so, when? If so, why?

Over delivering throughout the sale is crucial.

Over delivering after the sale is critical.

If you're selling using the principles I've shared with you, you're over delivering on character. Your character will be above and beyond what is expected. You will shine from the start. You also aren't expecting to be paid for over delivering. It's simply who you are and what you do.

Some salespeople will try to over deliver on the front end in an effort to manipulate the buyer into thinking they are better than they really are. That is not over delivering. That is manipulation. Your intention will determine if you're over delivering or if you're manipulating. If you're over delivering as a way to serve the buyer, it is over delivering. If you're over delivering as a way to get the sale, you're manipulating the buyer. The *why* or *intention* behind your actions determines if you're making deposits or withdrawals.

The most impactful way to over deliver is to do it after the sale. When it comes after the sale has been made, it's always seen as an expression of gratitude which is a great deposit. Gratitude motivates and inspires others to repeat the behavior we appreciated.

Over delivering after the sale doesn't have to be expensive. It's about creating an additional feeling, an emotion, a deeper connection to the buyer by leveraging the unexpected. It doesn't have to be something huge and difficult. It simply must be something unexpected that conveys your appreciation for their business.

Think back to my story about the M&Ms. That was a low cost form of over delivering which provided a big ROI for that company in the form of sales and *word of mouth*. It's an unexpected wash and vacuum when I drop my car off for an oil change or a tire rotation. It's a handwritten thank you note with a gift card. Could the gift be expensive or nice? Absolutely. It's up to you.

However, it's not about the value. It's about the intention behind it. The intention of conveying to the buyer: You matter. I value you. Thank you.

It's about the feeling YOU create in the buyer when they receive more than they expected or paid for. Get creative. If you're on a tight budget, don't let that stop you. It's worth repeating, *"With people, the small things are often the big things."* Often, the small things generate a deeper emotional tie than the big things.

Ria says it well, *"Giving an extra 'inch' will take you an extra mile."* The over deliver after the sale is one last opportunity to sell yourself using long term thinking. When you do something to create a strong, positive emotional feeling after the sale, you are guaranteed a full dose of *positive word of mouth* and repeat business.

The most important thing you will ever sell is yourself.

SELLER BEWARE
1. For the amateur, the payment ends the sale. For the pro, the over deliver strengthens the relationship.
2. Over delivering offers a HUGE competitive advantage. Are you leveraging over delivering? You should be!
3. You must be intentional about over delivering. Over deliver. Over deliver. Over deliver. Over delivering sells!

I welcome hearing how this book has influenced the way you think, the way you sell, or the results you have achieved because of what you've learned in it. Please feel free to share your thoughts with me by email at:

Mack@MackStory.com

To order my books, audio books, and other resources, please visit: TopStoryLeadership.com or Amazon.

ABOUT THE AUTHOR

Mack's story is an amazing journey of personal and professional growth. He married Ria in 2001. He has one son, Eric, born in 1991.

After graduating high school in 1987, Mack joined the United States Marine Corps Reserve as an 0311 infantryman. Soon after, he began his 20 plus year manufacturing career. Graduating with highest honors, he earned an Executive Bachelor of Business Administration degree from Faulkner University.

Mack began his career in manufacturing in 1988 on the front lines of a large production machine shop. He eventually grew himself into upper management and found his niche in lean manufacturing and along with it, developed his passion for leadership. In 2008, he launched his own Lean Manufacturing and Leadership Development firm.

From 2005-2012, Mack led leaders and their cross-functional teams through more than 11,000 hours of process improvement, organizational change, and cultural transformation. Ria joined Mack full-time in late 2013.

In 2013, they worked with John C. Maxwell as part of an international training event focused on the Cultural Transformation in Guatemala where over 20,000 leaders were trained. They also shared the stage with internationally recognized motivational speaker Les Brown in 2014.

Mack and Ria have published 20+ books on personal growth and leadership development and publish more each year. In 2018, they reached 66,000 international followers on LinkedIn where they provide daily motivational, inspirational, and leadership content to people all over the world.

Clients: ATD (Association for Talent Development), Auburn University, Chevron, Chick-fil-A, Kimberly Clark, Koch Industries, Southern Company, and the U.S. Military.

Mack is an inspiration for people everywhere as an example of achievement, growth, and personal development. His passion motivates and inspires people all over the world!

WHAT WE OFFER:

- ✓ Keynote Speaking: Conferences, Seminars, Onsite
- ✓ Workshops: Onsite/Offsite Half/Full/Multi Day
- ✓ Leadership Development Support: Leadership, Teamwork, Personal Growth, Organizational Change, Planning, Executing, Trust, Cultural Transformation, Communication, Time Management, Selling with Character, Resilience, & Relationship Building
- ✓ Blue-Collar Leadership® Development
- ✓ Corporate Retreats
- ✓ Women's Retreat (with Ria Story)
- ✓ Limited one-on-one coaching/mentoring
- ✓ On-site Lean Leadership Certification
- ✓ Lean Leader Leadership Development
- ✓ Become licensed to teach our content

FOR MORE INFORMATION PLEASE VISIT:

BlueCollarLeadership.com
TopStoryLeadership.com

FOLLOW US ON SOCIAL MEDIA:

LinkedIn.com/in/MackStory
Facebook.com/Mack.Story

LinkedIn.com/in/RiaStory
Facebook.com/Ria.Story

LISTEN/SUBSCRIBE TO OUR PODCASTS AT:

Mack Story: Anchor.fm/BlueCollarLeadership
Ria Story: Anchor.fm/RiaStory

Excerpt from

Defining Influence:
Increasing Your Influence Increases Your Options

In *Defining Influence*, I outline the foundational leadership principles and lessons we must learn in order to develop our character in a way that allows us to increase our influence with others. I also share many of my personal stories revealing how I got it wrong many times in the past and how I grew from front-line factory worker to become a Motivational Leadership Speaker.

INTRODUCTION

When You Increase Your Influence, You Increase Your Options.

"Leadership is influence. Nothing more. Nothing less. Everything rises and falls on leadership." ~ *John C. Maxwell*

Everyone is born a leader. However, everyone is not born a high impact leader.

I haven't always believed everyone is a leader. You may or may not at this point. That's okay. There is a lot to learn about leadership.

At this very moment, you may already be thinking to yourself, *"I'm not a leader."* My goal is to help you understand why everyone is a leader and to help you develop a deeper understanding of the principles of leadership and influence.

Developing a deep understanding of leadership has changed my life for the better. It has also changed the lives of my family members, friends, associates, and clients. My intention is to help you improve not only your life, but also the lives of those around you.

Until I became a student of leadership in 2008 which eventually led me to become a John Maxwell Certified Leadership Coach, Trainer, and Speaker in 2012, I did not understand leadership or realize everyone can benefit from learning the related principles.

In the past, I thought leadership was a term associated with being the boss and having formal authority over others. Those people are definitely leaders. But, I had been missing something. All of the other seven billion people on the planet are leaders too.

I say everyone is born a leader because I agree with John Maxwell, *"Leadership is Influence. Nothing more. Nothing less."* Everyone has influence. It's a fact. Therefore, everyone is a leader.

No matter your age, gender, religion, race, nationality, location, or position, everyone has influence. Whether you want to be a leader or not, you are. After reading this book, I hope you do not question whether or not you are a leader. However, I do hope you question what type of leader you are and what you need to do to increase your influence.

Everyone does not have authority, but everyone does have influence. There are plenty of examples in the world of people without authority leading people through influence alone. Actually, every one of us is an example. We have already done it. We know it is true. This principle is self-evident which means it contains its own evidence and does not need to be demonstrated or explained; it is obvious to everyone: we all have influence with others.

As I mentioned, the question to ask yourself is not, *"Am I a leader?"* The question to ask yourself is, *"What type of leader am I?"* The answer: whatever kind you choose to be. Choosing not to be a leader is not an option. As long as you live, you will have influence. You are a leader.

You started influencing your parents before you were actually born. You may have influence after your death. How? Thomas Edison still influences the world every time a light is turned on, you may do things in your life to influence others long after you're gone. Or, you may pass away with few people noticing. It depends on the choices you make.

Even when you're alone, you have influence.

The most important person you will ever influence is yourself. The degree to which you influence yourself determines the level of influence you ultimately have with others. Typically, when we are talking about leading ourselves, the word most commonly used to describe self-leadership is discipline which can be defined as giving yourself a command and following through with it. We must practice discipline daily to increase our influence with others.

> *"We must all suffer one of two things: the pain of discipline or the pain of regret or disappointment."* ~ *Jim Rohn*

As I define leadership as influence, keep in mind the words leadership and influence can be interchanged anytime and anywhere. They are one and the same. Throughout this book, I'll help you remember by placing one of the words in parentheses next to the other occasionally as a reminder. They are synonyms. When you read one, think of the other.

Everything rises and falls on influence (leadership). When you share what you're learning, clearly define leadership as influence for others. They need to understand the context of what you are teaching and understand they *are* leaders (people with influence) too. If you truly want to learn and apply leadership principles, you must start teaching this material to others within 24-48 hours of learning it yourself.

You will learn the foundational principles of leadership (influence) which will help you understand the importance of the following five questions. You will be able to take effective action by growing yourself and possibly others to a higher level of leadership (influence). Everything you ever achieve, internally and externally, will be a direct result of your influence.

1. ***Why*** **do we influence?** – Our character determines *why* we influence. Who we are on the inside is what matters. Do we manipulate or motivate? It's all about our intent.

2. ***How*** **do we influence?** – Our character, combined with our competency, determines *how* we influence. Who we are and what we know combine to create our unique style of influence which determines our methods of influence.

3. ***Where*** **do we influence?** – Our passion and purpose determine *where* we have the greatest influence. What motivates and inspires us gives us the energy and authenticity to motivate and inspire others.

4. ***Who*** **do we influence?** – We influence those *who* buy-in to us. Only those valuing and seeking what we value and seek will volunteer to follow us. They give us or deny us permission to influence them based on how well we have developed our character and competency.

5. **When do we influence?** – We influence others *when* they want our influence. We choose when others influence us. Everyone else has the same choice. They decide when to accept or reject our influence.

The first three questions are about the choices we make as we lead (influence) ourselves and others. The last two questions deal more with the choices others will make as they decide first, *if* they will follow us, and second, *when* they will follow us. They will base their choices on *who we are* and *what we know*.

Asking these questions is important. Knowing the answers is more important. But, taking action based on the answers is most important. Cumulatively, the answers to these questions determine our leadership style and our level of influence (leadership).

On a scale of 1-10, your influence can be very low level (1) to very high level (10). But make no mistake, you *are* a leader. You *are* always on the scale. There is a positive and negative scale too. The higher on the scale you are the more effective you are. You will be at different levels with different people at different times depending on many different variables.

Someone thinking they are not a leader or someone that doesn't want to be a leader is still a leader. They will simply remain a low impact leader with low level influence getting low level results. They will likely spend much time frustrated with many areas of their life. Although they could influence a change, they choose instead to be primarily influenced by others.

What separates high impact leaders from low impact leaders? There are many things, but two primary differences are:

1) High impact leaders accept more responsibility in all areas of their lives while low impact leaders tend to blame others and transfer responsibility more often.

2) High impact leaders have more positive influence while low impact leaders tend to have more negative influence.

My passion has led me to grow into my purpose which is to help others increase their influence personally and professionally while setting and reaching their goals. I am very passionate and have great conviction. I have realized many benefits by getting better results in all areas of my life. I have improved relationships with my family members, my friends, my associates, my peers, and my clients. I have witnessed people within these same groups embrace leadership principles and reap the same benefits.

The degree to which I *live* what I teach determines my effectiveness. My goal is to learn it, live it, and *then* teach it. I had major internal struggles as I grew my way to where I am. I'm a long way from perfect, so I seek daily improvement. Too often, I see people teaching leadership but not living what they're teaching. If I teach it, I live it.

My goal is to be a better leader tomorrow than I am today. I simply must get out of my own way and lead. I must lead me effectively before I can lead others effectively, not only with acquired knowledge, but also with experience from applying and living the principles.

I'll be transparent with personal stories to help you see how I have applied leadership principles by sharing: How I've struggled. How I've learned. How I've sacrificed. And, how I've succeeded.

Go beyond highlighting or underlining key points. Take the time to write down your thoughts related to the principle. Write down what you want to change. Write down how you can apply the principle in your life. You may want to consider getting a journal to fully capture your thoughts as you progress through the chapters. What you are thinking as you read is often much more important than what you're reading.

Most importantly, do not focus your thoughts on others. Yes, they need it too. We all need it. I need it. You need it. However, if you focus outside of yourself, you are missing the very point. Your influence comes from within. Your influence rises and falls based on your choices. You have untapped and unlimited potential waiting to be released. Only you can release it.

You, like everyone else, were born a leader. Now, let's take a leadership journey together.

(If you enjoyed this Introduction to *Defining Influence*, it is available in paperback, audio, and as an eBook on Amazon.com or for a signed copy you can purchase at TopStoryLeadership.com.)

Excerpt from

10 Values of High Impact Leaders

Our values are the foundation upon which we build our character. I'll be sharing 10 values high impact leaders work to master because they know these values will have a tremendous impact on their ability to lead others well. You may be thinking, *"Aren't there more than 10 leadership values?"* Absolutely! They seem to be endless. And, they are all important. These are simply 10 key values which I have chosen to highlight.

Since leadership is very dynamic and complex, the more values you have been able to internalize and utilize synergistically together, the more effective you will be. The more influence you will have.

"High performing organizations that continuously invest in leadership development are now defining new 21st century leadership models to deal with today's gaps in their leadership pipelines and the new global business environment. These people-focused organizations have generated nearly 60% improved business growth, reported a 66% improvement in bench strength, and showed a 62% improvement in employee retention. And, our research shows that it is not enough to just spend money on leadership training, but rather to follow specific practices that drive accelerated business results." ~ Josh Bersin

Do you want to become a high impact leader?

I believe everyone is a leader, but they are leading at different levels.

I believe everyone can and should lead from *where they are.*

I believe everyone can and should make a high impact.

I believe growth doesn't just happen; we must make it happen.

I believe before you will invest in yourself you must first believe in yourself.

I believe leaders must believe in their team before they will invest in their team.

I truly believe *everything rises and falls on influence.*

There is a story of a tourist who paused for a rest in a small town in the mountains. He went over to an old man sitting on a bench in front of the only store in town and inquired, *"Friend, can you tell me something this town is noted for?"*

"Well," replied the old man, *"I don't rightly know except it's the starting point to the world. You can start here and go anywhere you want."* [1]

That's a great little story. We are all at *"the starting point"* to the world, and we *"can start here and go anywhere we want."* We can expand our influence 360° in all directions by starting in the center with ourselves.

Consider the following illustration. Imagine you are standing in the center. You can make a high impact. However, it will not happen by accident. You must become intentional. You must live with purpose while focusing on your performance as you develop your potential.

Note: Illustration and 10 Values are listed on the following pages.

Why we do what we do is about our *purpose.*

How we do what we do is about our *performance.*

What we do will determine our *potential.*

Where these three components overlap, you will achieve a
HIGH IMPACT.

10 Values of High Impact Leaders

1

THE VALUE OF VISION
Vision is the foundation of hope.
"When there's hope in the future, there's power in the present." ~ Les Brown

2

THE VALUE OF MODELING
Someone is always watching you.
"Who we are on the inside is what people see on the outside." ~ Mack Story

3

THE VALUE OF RESPONSIBILITY
When we take responsibility, we take control.
"What is common sense is not always common practice." ~ Stephen R. Covey

4

THE VALUE OF TIMING
It matters when you do what you do.
"It's about doing the right thing for the right reason at the right time." ~ Mack Story

5

THE VALUE OF RESPECT
To be respected, we must be respectful.
"Go See, ask why, and show respect"
~ Jim Womack

6

THE VALUE OF EMPOWERMENT
***Leaders gain influence by
giving it to others.***
"Leadership is not reserved for leaders."
~ Marcus Buckingham

7

THE VALUE OF DELEGATION
***We should lead with questions
instead of directions.***
*"Delegation 101: Delegating 'what to do,' makes
you responsible. Delegating 'what to accomplish,'
allows others to become responsible."*
~ Mack Story

8

THE VALUE OF MULTIPLICATION
None of us is as influential as all of us.
*"To add growth, lead followers. To multiply, lead
leaders." ~ John C. Maxwell*

9

THE VALUE OF RESULTS
Leaders like to make things happen.
"Most people fail in the getting started."
~ Maureen Falcone

10

THE VALUE OF SIGNIFICANCE
Are you going to settle for success?
"Significance is a choice that only
successful people can make."
~ Mack Story

Order books online at Amazon or TopStoryLeadership.com

High impact leaders align their habits with key values in order to maximize their influence. High impact leaders intentionally grow and develop themselves in an effort to more effectively grow and develop others.

These *10 Values* are commonly understood. However, they are not always commonly practiced. These *10 Values* will help you build trust and accelerate relationship building. Those mastering these *10 Values* will be able to lead with speed as they develop 360° of influence from wherever they are.

Order books online at Amazon or TopStoryLeadership.com

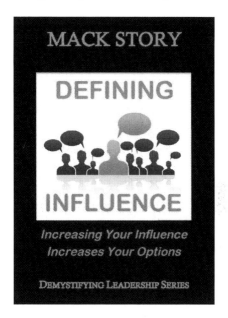

Are you looking for transformation in your life? Do you want better results? Do you want stronger relationships?

In *Defining Influence*, Mack breaks down many of the principles that will allow anyone at any level to methodically and intentionally increase their positive influence.

Mack blends his personal growth journey with lessons on the principles he learned along the way. He's not telling you what he learned after years of research, but rather what he learned from years of application and transformation. Everything rises and falls on influence.

Order books online at Amazon or TopStoryLeadership.com

10 Foundational Elements of Intentional Transformation serves as a source of motivation and inspiration to help you climb your way to the next level and beyond as you learn to intentionally create a better future for yourself. The pages will ENCOURAGE, ENGAGE, and EMPOWER you as you become more focused and intentional about moving from where you are to where you want to be.

All of us are somewhere, but most of us want to be somewhere else. However, we don't always know how to get there. You will learn how to intentionally move forward as you learn to navigate the 10 foundational layers of transformation.

Order books online at Amazon or BlueCollarLeadership.com

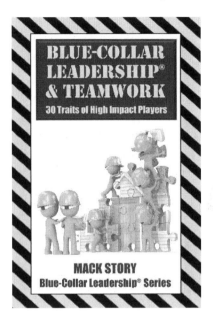

Are you ready to play at the next level and beyond?

In today's high stakes game of business, the players on the team are the competitive advantage for any organization. But, only if they are on the field instead of on the bench.

The competitive advantage for every individual is developing 360° of influence regardless of position, title, or rank.

Blue-Collar Leadership® & Teamwork provides a simple, yet powerful and unique, resource for individuals who want to increase their influence and make a high impact. It's also a resource and tool for leaders, teams, and organizations, who are ready to Engage the Front Line to Improve the Bottom Line.

Order books online at Amazon or BlueCollarLeadership.com

"I wish someone had given me these books 30 years ago when I started my career on the front lines. They would have changed my life then. They can change your life now." ~ Mack Story

Blue-Collar Leadership® & Supervision and *Blue-Collar Leadership®* are written specifically for those who lead the people on the frontlines and for those on the front lines. With 30 short, easy to read 3 page chapters, these books contain powerful, yet simple to understand leadership lessons.

Note: These two Blue-Collar Leadership® books are the blue-collar version of the MAXIMIZE books and contain nearly identical content.

Down load the first 5 chapters of each book FREE at: BlueCollarLeadership.com

Order books online at Amazon or BlueCollarLeadership.com

The biggest challenge in process improvement and cultural transformation isn't identifying the problems. It's execution: implementing and sustaining the solutions.

Blue-Collar Kaizen is a resource for anyone in any position who is, or will be, leading a team through process improvement and change. Learn to engage, empower, and encourage your team for long term buy-in and sustained gains.

Mack Story has over 11,000 hours experience leading hundreds of leaders and thousands of their cross-functional kaizen team members through process improvement, organizational change, and cultural transformation. He shares lessons learned from his experience and many years of studying, teaching, and applying leadership principles.

Order books online at Amazon or TopStoryLeadership.com

"I wish someone had given me these books 30 years ago when I started my career. They would have changed my life then. They can change your life now." ~ Mack Story

MAXIMIZE Your Potential will help you learn to lead yourself well. *MAXIMIZE Your Leadership Potential* will help you learn to lead others well. With 30 short, easy to read 3 page chapters, these books contain simple and easy to understand, yet powerful leadership lessons.

Note: These two MAXIMIZE books are the white-collar, or non-specific, version of the Blue-Collar Leadership® books and contain nearly identical content.

ABOUT RIA STORY

Mack's wife, Ria, is also a motivational leadership speaker, author, and a world class coach who has a unique ability to help people develop and achieve their life and career goals, and guide them in building the habits and discipline to achieve their personal view of greatness. Ria brings a wealth of personal experience in working with clients to achieve their personal goals and aspirations in a way few coaches can.

Like many, Ria has faced adversity in life. Raised on an isolated farm in Alabama, she suffered extreme sexual abuse by her father from age 12 to 19. Desperate to escape, she left home at 19 without a job, a car, or even a high school diploma. Ria learned to be resilient, and not just survive, but thrive. (Watch her 7 minute TEDx talk at RiaStory.com/TEDx) She worked her way through school, acquiring an MBA with a 4.0 GPA, and eventually resigned from her career in the corporate world to pursue a passion for helping others achieve success.

Ria's background includes more than 10 years in healthcare administration, including several years in management, and later, Director of Compliance and Regulatory Affairs for a large healthcare organization. Ria's responsibilities included oversight of thousands of organizational policies, organizational compliance with all State and Federal regulations, and responsibility for several million dollars in Medicare appeals.

Ria co-founded Top Story Leadership, which offers leadership speaking, training, coaching, and consulting.

Ria's Story From Ashes To Beauty
by Ria Story

The unforgettable story and inspirational memoir of a young woman who was extremely sexually abused by her father from age 12 to 19 and then rejected by her mother. (Watch 7 minutes of her story in her TEDx talk at RiaStory.com/TEDx)

For the first time, Ria publicly reveals details of the extreme sexual abuse she endured growing up. 13 years after leaving home at 19, she decided to speak out about her story and encourage others to find hope and healing.

Determined to not only survive, but also thrive, Ria shares how she was able to overcome the odds and find hope and healing to Achieve Abundant Life. She shares the leadership principles she applied to find professional success, personal significance, and details how she was able to find the courage to share her story to give hope to others around the world.

Ria states, *"It would be easier for me to let this story go untold forever and simply move on with life…One of the most difficult things I've ever done is write this book. Victims of sexual assault or abuse don't want to talk because they want to avoid the social stigma and the fear of not being believed or the possibility of being blamed for something that was not their fault. My hope and prayer is someone will benefit from learning how I was able to overcome such difficult circumstances. That brings purpose to the pain and reason enough to share what I would rather have left behind forever. Our scars make us stronger."*

Available at Amazon.com in paperback, audio, and eBook. To order your signed copy, to learn more about Ria, or to book her to speak at your event, please visit: RiaStory.com/TEDx

Order books online at Amazon or RiaStory.com

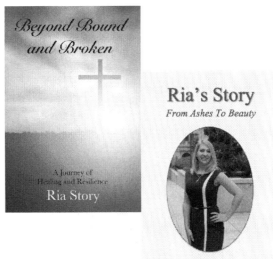

In *Beyond Bound and Broken*, Ria shares how she overcame the shame, fear, and doubt she developed after enduring years of extreme sexual abuse by her father. Forced to play the role of a wife and even shared with other men due to her father's perversions, Ria left home at 19 without a job, a car, or even a high-school diploma. This book also contains lessons on resilience and overcoming adversity that you can apply to your own life.

In *Ria's Story From Ashes To Beauty*, Ria tells her personal story of growing up as a victim of extreme sexual abuse from age 12 – 19, leaving home to escape, and her decision to tell her story. She shares her heart in an attempt to help others overcome their own adversity.

Order books online at Amazon or RiaStory.com

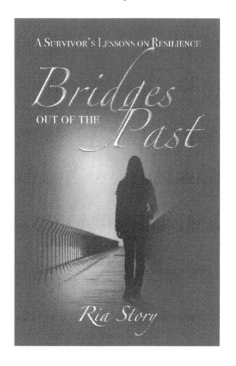

It's not what happens to you in life. It's who you become because of it. We all experience pain, grief, and loss in life. Resilience is the difference between *"I didn't die,"* and *"I learned to live again."* In this captivating book on resilience, Ria walks you through her own horrific story of more than seven years of sexual abuse by her father. She then shares how she learned not only to survive, but also to thrive in spite of her past. Learn how to overcome challenges, obstacles, and adversity in your own life by building a bridge out of the past and into the future.

(Watch 7 minutes of her story at RiaStory.com/TEDx)

Order books online at Amazon or RiaStory.com

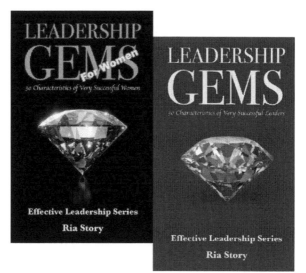

Note: Leadership Gems is the generic, non-gender specific, version of Leadership Gems for Women. The content is very similar.

Women are naturally high level leaders because they are relationship oriented. However, it's a *"man's world"* out there and natural ability isn't enough to help you be successful as a leader. You must be intentional.

Ria packed these books with 30 leadership gems which very successful people internalize and apply. Ria has combined her years of experience in leadership roles of different organizations along with years of studying, teaching, training, and speaking on leadership to give you these 30, short and simple, yet powerful and profound, lessons to help you become very successful, regardless of whether you are in a formal leadership position or not.

Order books online at Amazon or RiaStory.com

Become inspired by this 30-day collection of daily devotions for women, where you will find practical advice on intentionally living with a grateful heart, inspirational quotes, short journaling opportunities, and scripture from God's Word on practicing gratitude.

Order books online at Amazon or RiaStory.com

Ria's *Effective Leadership Series* books are written to develop and enhance your leadership skills, while also helping you increase your abilities in areas like communication and relationships, time management, planning and execution, leading and implementing change. Look for more books in the *Effective Leadership Series*:

- *Straight Talk: The Power of Effective Communication*

- *PRIME Time: The Power of Effective Planning*

- *Change Happens: Leading Yourself and Others through Change (Co-authored by Ria & Mack Story)*

Made in the USA
Columbia, SC
03 March 2019